Shiga Naoya

(TWAS 319)

Shiga Naoya

Shiga Naoya

By FRANCIS MATHY

Sophia University, Tokyo

Twayne Publishers, Inc. :: New York

Library of Congress Cataloging in Publication Data

Mathy, Francis.
  Shiga Naoya.

  (Twayne's world authors series, TWAS 319.   Japan.)
  1.   Shiga, Naoya, 1883-1971.
PL816.H5Z75   895.6'3'3   74-1448
ISBN 0-8057-2648-9

MANUFACTURED IN THE UNITED STATES OF AMERICA

Contents

92220

About the Author

Francis Mathy is a Catholic priest of the Society of Jesus and professor of English and Japanese literature at Sophia University in Tokyo. While teaching English and American literature to Japanese students in the Japanese division of the university, he also lectures on Japanese literature to the foreign students of the international division. He obtained a Ph.D. in Comparative Literature from the University of Michigan in 1963 and wrote his dissertation on the Japanese writer of the Meiji period, Kitamura Tokoku. He has had articles published in *Comparative Literature*, *Monumenta Nipponica*, *Thought*, and *Hikaku bungaku*, the Japanese journal of comparative literature. He is the translator of Natsume Soseki's *Mon* and Endo Shusaku's *Ogon on kuni* (The Golden Country) and *Obaka san* (Wonderful Fool).

Preface

Shiga Naoya is a man of paradox. At the time of his death in 1971 at
the age of eighty-eight he was the oldest living Japanese writer of
name. Yet except for the concluding section of his one full-length
novel, *Journey Through Dark Night,* published in 1937, he had
completed all his significant work by 1928. His writing after this
date one critic has compared to the occasional sputtering of a dead
volcano. Moreover, even in his most active period, the two decades
between 1908 and 1928, he was never prolific and suffered through
long stretches of dryness when he was unable to write. The body of
his work consists of one long novel, several long stories, a number of
shorter stories, and a host of sketches and essays.

Shiga holds a position in the history of modern Japanese
literature greatly disproportionate to the slender volume of his
work. Writers of very different schools of writing have paid tribute
to him and acknowledged his influence. Akutagawa Ryunosuke,
himself one of the finest of Japanese short-story writers, considered
Shiga to be the better writer. Though the Shirakaba school of
writers to which Shiga belonged began as a reaction to the prevailing Naturalistic trend in literature, Naturalist writers, such as
Kobayashi Takiji, were equally fervent in his praise and found in his
realism a means of escape from the narrowness of their own writing.
Tanizaki Junichiro, Kawabata Yasunari, Yokomitsu Riiichi, Niwa
Fumio, and many other writers were among his admirers. Not even
the two greatest literary figures of modern Japanese literature, Natsume Soseki and Mori Ogai, states the critic Nakamura Mitsuo,
have had greater influence. Thus, he has been called the
"hometown" of modern Japanese literature, one of the foundation
stones of that literature, and even "a god of the novel." In justifica-
tion for this last epithet, the critic Yoshida Ken'ichi asserts that
Shiga's works have a certain classical quality so that however often
one turns to them, one always finds there something fresh and new,
and Shiga is the only living writer (1949) of whom this can be said.

The Western reader approaching Shiga may well find it hard to
understand why he is held in such high regard. Reading through his
work, he may not find much to indicate that Shiga is more than a

good minor writer who has written a handful of excellent short stories—among the best in Japanese literature—and a number of fine lyrical sketches. His one novel, if such it can be called, is poorly organized, has little or no characterization, and is so narrowly focused on the microscopic world of the central character that the reader feels something akin to claustrophobia. Much the same can be said for the greater part of his autobiographical "fiction."

It is true that postwar writers and critics have made a much less favorable reassessment of Shiga's significance. Four prominent novelists in a discussion of him in the magazine *Bungei* in 1949 do in fact relegate him to the position of a minor writer and express wonder that the previous generation of writers should have stood in such awe of him, and they rejoice that they have been liberated from the authority of "this avatar of the deity." Yet as we read on we see that their liberation is not all that complete. The four admit, for example, that "when Edward Seidensticker and other American scholars say that they do not understand why Shiga is esteemed so highly or even how his work can be called fiction, we bristle. We feel that he cannot be dismissed so simply."[1] They go on to speculate that the reason for this reaction is that Shiga possesses some element that is very much a part of the Japanese bloodstream, that his work is closely connected with the Oriental view of life.

It is no easy matter, then, to do an objective study of a writer like Shiga. It will be necessary to keep a double focus: to try to understand what Shiga means to the Japanese and why; and at the same time not to neglect the task of critical appraisal, not to fail to answer one of the most important questions to be asked concerning the writer of another literature—that is, how universal is his work, what does it contribute to world literature? In this study we shall often take into consideration the appraisal of the Japanese critics as well as present our own. We will do our best at the end to harmonize the two views, attempting to find an explanation for divergences of opinion.

One further characteristic of this study is that we will quote Shiga himself at greater length than would be necessary if more of his work were available in English translation. In this way the reader will be better able to judge for himself the merit of the critical opinions expressed. But here a warning is in order. The one point on which all critics are agreed is that of the excellence of Shiga's style.

Preface

He is one of the most difficult of Japanese writers to translate. Professor Valdo Viglielmo after beginning a translation of *Journey Through Dark Night* discovered that "try as I might, the English that emerged was but a pallid reflection of the original. . . . It was as if Shiga's style was such a rare and subtle perfume that it evaporated as I transferred it from one bottle to another."[2]

Finally, we express the hope that this study will contribute not only to an understanding of Shiga Naoya but also to a better realization of some of the unique qualities of Japanese literature.

Francis Mathy, S. J.

Sophia University, Tokyo

Note

It seems well at the outset to list the titles of Shiga's works that will be referred to in this study together with their English translations, so that hereafter only the English title need be used. The following list is chronological.

"Aru asa"	"One Morning"
"Abashiri made"	"To Abashiri"
"Aru ichipeiji"	"One Page"
"Kamisori"	"The Razor"
"Nigotta atama"	"Confused Head"
"Rojin"	"The Old Man"
"Sobo no tame ni"	"For Grandmother"
"Haha no shi to atarashii haha"	"My Mother's Death and the Coming of My New Mother"
"Otsu Junkichi"	"Otsu Junkichi"
"Seigi-ha"	"The Just Ones"
"Kurodeias no nikki"	"Claudius's Journal"
"Seibei to hyotan"	"Seibei's Gourds"
"Haha no shi to tabi no kioku"	"Recollections of My Mother's Death and of Her Tabi"
"Dekigoto"	"An Incident"
"Han no hanzai"	"Han's Crime"
"Ko o nusumu hanashi"	"The Kidnapping"
"Gukyo"	"My Temporary Dwelling"
"Tombo"	"Dragonfly"
"Yamori"	"Wall Lizard"
"Yadokari no shi"	"Hermit Crab"
"Arashi no hi"	"Day of Storm"
"Yama no ki to oga"	"The Mountain Tree and the Giant Saw"
"Kinosaki nite"	"At Kinosaki"
"Kojinbutsu no fufu"	"The Good-Natured Couple"
"Akanishi Kakita"	"Akanishi Kakita"
"Wakai"	"Reconciliation"

Note

The text of Shiga's work used for this study is that of the 1955 Iwanami edition in seventeen volumes. All translations, unless otherwise indicated, are my own. The number given after each translated passage is a reference to volume and page of the Iwanami text.

In preparing this study I have made use of many books and essays on Shiga (see the notes and bibliography), but the following three have been particularly helpful: Nakamura Mitsuo's *Shiga Naoya ron*, Sudo Matsuo's *Shiga Naoya no bungaku,* and the collection of essays on Shiga put together in the *Nihon bungaku kenkyu shiryo sosho* series.

I wish to thank Mr. Edmund Skrzypczak for going over the manuscript and suggesting a number of improvements, and Professor Roy Teele for his careful editing.

Chronology

1883   Shiga Naoya born February 20 in the town of Ishimaki in Miyagi Prefecture.

1885   Family moves to Tokyo and takes up residence with grandparents.

1889   Enters Gakushuin Elementary School.

1895   Advances to Gakushuin Middle School. Mother dies. Father remarries.

1900   Begins to study Christianity under the tutelage of Uchimura Kanzo.

1901   Has a falling-out with his father over the Ashio Copper Mine pollution incident.

1902   Fails the year at Gakushuin (for the second time) and is unable to graduate from middle school. Finds himself in the same class as Mushakoji Saneatsu.

1903   Advances to Gakushuin High School.

1906   Grandfather dies. Enters the English literature department of Tokyo Imperial University.

1907   Becomes a member of the Fortnight Club, the nucleus for the later Shirakaba group. Proposes to marry one of the family maids but is opposed by the entire family.

1908   Writes "One Morning" and four other stories. With Mushakoji and others begins the magazine that is to develop into *Shirakaba*. Transfers to the Japanese literature department of the university but does not attend classes. Breaks away from Uchimura Kanzo.

1910   Writes "The Razor" and "Confused Head." Joins with Mushakoji, the Arishima brothers, Satomi Ton, and others to begin the magazine *Shirakaba*. Formally withdraws from university.

1911   Writes "The Old Man" and "For Grandmother."

1912   Writes "My Mother's Death and the Coming of My New Mother," "Otsu Junkichi," "The Just Ones," "Claudius's Journal," "Seibei's Gourds." Relationship with father grows worse and Shiga moves to Onomichi where he begins work on a long novel, *Tokito Kensaku*, which eventually becomes

Journey Through Dark Night.

1913   Writes "An Incident" and "Han's Crime" and publishes the first collection of his stories. On a visit to Tokyo is hit by a streetcar and seriously injured. Goes to Kinosaki Hot Springs to convalesce. Asked by Natsume Soseki to write a novel for serialization in the *Asahi News.*

1914   Writes "The Kidnapping." Spends the summer in Matsue, where he visits Mt. Daisen. Informs Soseki that he cannot write the promised novel. Moves to Kyoto in September and in December marries a cousin of Mushakoji, without his father's consent. Finds it impossible to write. For the next three years finishes only five short nature sketches.

1915   Moves first to Kamakura, then to Mt. Akagi, and finally to Abiko, where he lives for the next seven years.

1916   Daughter born but dies shortly after birth. Mushakoji moves to Abiko.

1917   Writes "At Kinosaki," "The Good-Natured Couple," "Reconciliation," and several other stories and sketches. Birth of second daughter and reconciliation with father.

1919   Writes "The Apprentice's God." Son born but dies a month later.

1920   Writes "A Certain Man and the Death of His Sister," "Bonfire," and "Manazuru." Another daughter born. (Four additional daughters and one son were later born to complete his family.)

1921   Publishes the first part of *Journey Through Dark Night.* Grandmother dies.

1922   Begins to publish the second half of *Journey Through Dark Night.*

1923   Moves to Kyoto and becomes absorbed in Oriental art. *Shirakaba* stops publication after the great earthquake of this year.

1925   Writes the Yamashina stories.

1926   Begins to complete *Journey Through Dark Night.*

1927   Writes "Kuniko."

1929   Writes "The Harvest Bugs." Father dies. Travels to Manchuria and Northern China. Takes up residence in Nara.

1931   Writes "Rhythm." First publication of his complete works in eight volumes.

Chronology

1937 Finally completes *Journey Through Dark Night.* Second publication of his complete works in nine volumes.

1938 Moves back to Tokyo.

1946 Writes "Ash-Colored Moon."

1947 Chosen as president of the Japan P.E.N. Club.

1952 Travels to Europe.

1955 Third publication of his complete works in seventeen volumes.

1966 *The White Line* and *Animal Sketches,* collections of his later pieces, published.

1971 Dies on October 21 of pneumonia and old age.

CHAPTER 1

Biographical Sketch

I Family and Childhood

S HIGA Naoya's long life was a singularly uneventful one. There was very little that could be called drama in it. Yet it may more truly be said of him than of most writers that the nature and events of his life provided the basic material for his work. He never departed far from what he himself had personally experienced—what he had seen and heard, touched and felt. He stands at furthest remove from Henry James's art of fiction: he was never willing, nor indeed able, to construct a story from hints, notes, or suggestions gathered from here and there. He would not have understood what Graham Greene meant when he wrote, in the prefatory dedication to *The Comedians*, that the narrator of his tale was not himself, that "a physical trait taken here, a habit of speech, an anecdote—they are boiled up in the kitchen of the unconscious and emerge unrecognizable even to the cook in most cases." On the contrary, Shiga's life presents the most helpful clue to his works, and they in turn all but constitute his autobiography.

He was born February 20, 1883, in a little village in northern Honshu, where his father, then thirty-one, was employed at a bank. Before he was three, however, the family moved to Tokyo, taking up residence with his father's parents, so that Shiga's earliest memories are of Tokyo, where he remained until he reached manhood.

Shiga's family had for generations been samurai retainers of the Soma clan. After the disbanding of the clan, Naoya's grandfather had become administrator of the dwindling finances of the Soma family. Naoya's father, on the other hand, accommodating himself to the spirit of the times, embarked upon a career in the business world. After graduating from Keio Gijuku (the present Keio University) he was employed by the Dai-ichi Bank and sent to several branch offices in the provinces. In 1885 he resigned from the bank to accept a very good position with a Tokyo firm, and he later became director of two other companies. He proved himself to be an enterprising and eminently successful businessman, so that Naoya had never to worry about financial support and could pursue his literary ambitions without the fear of not being able to support himself as a writer.

From the moment of the removal to Tokyo, the raising of Naoya was taken over entirely by his grandparents. Naoya had had an older brother who had died of dysentery in his third year, the year before Naoya was born. The grandparents tended to place the blame for the untimely death of their first grandson on the parents, so that when their son and his family came to live with them, they immediately took over responsibility for Naoya. Naoya's mother lived in another house in the same compound and his father was away on business trips for the greater part of the year.

Naoya loved and admired his grandfather very much. He later named him one of the three people who had had the greatest influence on his life. (The other two were the Christian evangelist Uchimura Kanzo and his fellow writer Mushakoji Saneatsu.) The grandfather was undisputed head of the family and seems to have exercised his authority in the best samurai tradition—that is, with all the virtues of that tradition. There emanated from him always, Shiga states, an atmosphere of calm and serenity. The literary critic Nakamura Mitsuo points out, however, that the grandfather's influence may not have been all to the good: it may have congealed his grandson's spirit within too narrow a circle. Shiga at one time in his life, as we shall see, showed a great interest in social issues, even to the point of bitterly attacking his father and the capitalistic system he represented. But this interest never developed into a social philosophy, as it did for many of his fellow writers. He soon lost all interest in society as such and chose instead to concentrate his energies on "living sincerely." Even his rebellion against his father never developed into a rebellion against the feudal concept of family. Nakamura thinks that the lack of a social dimension in Shiga's thought and writing is due in great part to this strong influence from Japan's feudal past, that it was because of the commanding presence of his grandfather that his rebellion never developed into a view of society but remained confined to the realm of emotion.[1]

Until her death in 1921 at the age of eighty-six, Shiga was closer to his grandmother than to anyone else in the family, but her overindulgent love too was not without its bad effects. It accounted in great part for Naoya's willfulness and egoism, continuing even into adult life.

The death of Naoya's mother when he was thirteen was the first sorrowful event of his life. He was fortunate, however, in his father's choice of a successor. This extraordinary woman treated Naoya as her own child; and Naoya, willful and irascible as he was, seems always to have been on the best of terms with her and to have had a deep affection for her and the brother and five sisters she gave him. In all the stories in which she appears she is always a gentle presence, pouring oil upon the waters, especially at the worst period of Naoya's conflict with his father. One of the best of his stories tells of the death of his mother and the coming into the family of his stepmother.

At the age of six Shiga entered Gakushuin Elementary School, which was then known as Peers' School, and he continued there through middle and high school. A far better sportsman than student, he was particularly fond of gymnastics, boating, and cycling, but he was also good at baseball, tennis, and swimming. He did poorly in his studies, especially in language and literature, and twice had to repeat a year. Like most boys, he considered many different vocations—naval officer, businessman, philosopher, Christian evangelist—before he finally settled upon becoming a writer.

In 1900, at the age of seventeen, Shiga passed for the first time through the gate of the great Meiji Christian evangelist Uchimura Kanzo. He remained a disciple of Uchimura's for seven years. He confesses, however, that he was more deeply impressed with the man than with his teachings. In his essay "Recollections of Uchimura Kanzo" he writes:

I spent over seven years with Uchimura, but I was never a very good disciple, I'm afraid. The teachings, which for Uchimura were the main thing, never really became part of me. Since those days I have become a novelist of sorts, but I am extremely grateful that I learned from him to love what is right and hate what is wrong. Moreover, the fact that I was not willfully guilty of serious misdemeanor in those several years before and after my twentieth birthday, when temptations were so great, is due to the Christianity I learned from Uchimura. (IX, 211)

The young man Otsu Junkichi, in Shiga's story of that title, states that he was not inclined to find fault with Uchimura's teaching. He regarded him as a great thinker and was content to entrust himself to him. He was particularly attracted to the man's face—"dark-skinned, all the features on a large scale, awe-inspiring and yet affectionate, with eyes sharp and deep, looking as if they had been chiseled into the sides of his high nose bridge" (VI, 9). Junkichi thought that Uchimura had the finest face in Japan.

II *Conflict with Father*

Naoya's first great clash with his father took place shortly after he had become a disciple of Uchimura Kanzo. His father, as we have seen, was away from home for long periods while Naoya was grow-ing up, and probably never seemed much like a father to him.. There had been many angry exchanges of words before, but this was the first major confrontation. The point of conflict, considering Shiga's later development, was a most unlikely one.

In 1901, people living along the Watarase River, the river that flows between Gumma and Tochigi prefectures, came down with what was soon diagnosed as copper poisoning, and the source of the poisoning was traced to the waste liquids poured into the river by the Ashio Copper Mine. This pollution incident was immediately taken up as a big social issue, and some of the greatest men of the day, including Uchimura Kanzo, raised their voices in protest against capitalist irresponsibility. Aroused by the rhetoric of a protest rally, Shiga determined to go and inspect the site. His father, learning of his intention, flew into a rage and vehemently opposed his going.

What Shiga did not know at the time was that his own grand-father, when he was still in charge of the Soma finances, had been one of those responsible for the opening of the mine. Though he had made no personal profit from the enterprise and had since withdrawn himself from it, he had at the time of withdrawal re-ceived a considerable gift of money from the present owner. It was natural that Shiga's father should do his best to keep his son from becoming a source of embarrassment to the family. Moreover, conservative businessman that he was, he seems to have feared his son's getting involved with socialism. Shiga was incensed at his father's attitude and quarreled vehemently with him. In the event, however, he did not go through with his plan. Instead his mother and grandmother made up packages of food and clothing to be sent to the afflicted.

The second battle between father and son took place in 1907 when Shiga fell in love with one of the maids serving the family and set his mind upon marrying her. Both his father and his grandmother were strongly opposed to this, saying that no Shiga had ever contracted such a marriage. This affair constitutes the plot of his long story "Otsu Junkichi," and will be discussed at greater length later. The father got the girl out of the house, and though Naoya wrote to her for a time and even went to see her twice in her native village, the affair died a natural death. Shiga was soon taken up with other interests.

At the height of this affair with the maid, Shiga went to consult Uchimura Kanzo. He confessed to him that, unknown to the family, he was already living with the girl. Uchimura replied that it was a grievous sin to enter upon such a clandestine relationship with a woman that could not be openly acknowledged as his wife. For quite a while prior to this consultation Shiga had been experiencing great difficulty in reconciling Christian teaching on chastity as interpreted by Uchimura with his own strong sexual desires. This response of his mentor forced him to a decision with regard to Christianity. He thought the matter over for some time and then "I went to tell him that I would no longer be coming to his meetings. In fact, I never went there again. I did not feel the least compunction in leaving him. . . . I had now come to understand the path I must take, stumble along it though I might. That was why I felt I had to leave him."[2] Several months later Shiga published his first short story, "One Morning," and was on his way to success as a writer.

Shiga's decision to become a writer precipitated still another storm in the family. It is not hard to imagine the horror with which the successful businessman looked upon his son's determination to devote his life to writing, all the more since the son himself was doubtful that he would ever be able to make a living at it. The father was already greatly displeased with his son's manner of life. By this time, 1910, Naoya had dropped out of Tokyo Imperial University where he had matriculated upon graduation from Gakushuin, and was spending his days in what seemed to his father irresponsible idleness. It is not surprising that Naoya's father was disgusted with the disorder and seeming meaninglessness of his son's life. Naoya was now, after all, a man of twenty-seven, and still completely dependent upon his father.

III   *Decision to Become a Writer*

Though he did not do well in his studies, Shiga discovered the joys of reading very early in life. He does not seem to have considered the possibility of becoming a writer himself, however, until his final year of high school. Of the growth of his literary ambitions, he writes:

I became a writer for no other reason than that I liked to write. From about my thirteenth year I read everything I could get my hands on. But I didn't consider then becoming a writer, perhaps because I didn't think I had it in me. At first I thought of joining the Navy and then of becoming a prosperous businessman. Looking back now, I think I first thought seriously of writing as an occupation after I had begun to frequent Uchimura Kanzo's. This was probably because a career in the Navy or as a businessman, spending my life making money, came to seem so senseless. (XI, 140)

Chance played an important role in the decision. Upon failing for the second time to move up into the next grade at Gakushuin, he found himself in the same class with Mushakoji Saneatsu and several other young men who had already decided to devote their lives to writing. These young men encouraged each other and created the kind of atmosphere in which it seemed natural enough for Shiga too to decide upon a literary career.

This association continued after the students had gone on to college. At Tokyo Imperial University Shiga, who was enrolled in the English department, and Mushakoji, who was in the German, together with two other friends from Gakushuin, started a writing club and began a literary magazine. A short time later this magazine was combined with two others, efforts of Gakushuin graduates of other years, and the magazine *Shirakaba* (White

Birch), which was to give its name to this group of writers, was born. The first issue came out in April of 1910 and contained Shiga's story "To Abashiri." Other stories of his appeared in subsequent issues.

The Shirakaba writers were all men of good family and of sufficient financial means not to have to worry about their livelihood. They sought to develop their individual selves and to find within the self the ultimate value of life. This ideal appealed very much to Shiga, who at the time was very much concerned with the problem of self-realization. Much of his early work, in fact, can best be seen as a "song of self." But despite his self-absorption, affirmation of self did not come easily for him. He alternated between periods of exalted self-confidence and other periods of bitter discouragement and self-disparagement. This inability to achieve a steady view of self was undoubtedly an important factor in his long-continuing conflict with his father and his general surliness in the family circle. The morbidity of several of his stories of the years 1910 and 1911—particularly "The Razor," "Confused Head," and "For Grandmother"—give evidence of the tremendous strain upon his nervous system of this continued inward and outward struggle.

IV   *First Years of Taisho*

The opening years of the new era of Taisho, 1912, 1913, and 1914, were the most important years of Shiga's life as a writer. It was during this period that his internal and external struggle toward self-definition reached its highest crest and began to recede into that harmony that was to characterize the many decades still lying before him. It is not too much to say that it is the drama of these three years that fixed, for better or for worse, the essential character of his writing.

The year 1912 found Shiga at the highest tide of his bold confrontation with his father and also of his determination to make something of himself. In his journal for March of that year, we find the following two entries:

In the train I read Rousseau. . . . I do not know whether Rousseau is a great man or not. I don't think he is so very great, I thought that I, even as I am at present, have as much in me as Rousseau. In fact, in some ways I am better than he is, I thought. Man must spend his life—at least, I must spend my life in bringing out what is in me. I must mine what is in me. (March 7, 1912)

I have come to love myself with a deep love. I have come to feel that my face is really beautiful. I have come to believe that few people are as great as I am. I must spend my whole life in mining that in me which is lovable, beautiful, and great. (March 8, 1912) (XII, 223–24)

It is necessary to remind ourselves that the author of these lines was not a callow youth of fifteen or sixteen but a grown man of twenty-nine. As with the adolescent trying to achieve a steady view of himself as a unique person, so with Shiga too at this time the opposing mood of discouragement and self-disparagement was never far away. In the autobiographical "Otsu Junkichi," written in this same year, the hero says of himself:

[To my family] I probably appear to be no more than a child who has had a bad upbringing. They have no choice but to conclude that my proposals are never more than impracticable dreams, with no connection to real life. I am always impelled to say things that smack of a strong conceit. I realize there is a lack of balance between the burning ambition I have for my writing and the actual confidence I am able to muster in it. In short, up to the present I have written nothing that could justify even a little self-confidence. In spite of my self-importance all that has come out of me has been but a thin sound. A sound thin and shrill. And this shrill note of vainglory has not traveled beyond the ears of my intimate friends. Except to my friends, I have sounded like a demented fool. (VI, 64)

Thus Shiga, sharing the Shirakaba view of the supreme significance of the self, exalted his own self and its potentialities; but he experienced at the same time periods of great depression when it seemed that he was good for absolutely nothing. He often moved very quickly from one extreme of mood to the other. A further complicating element was the growing pressure of his sexual urges, which were rapidly getting out of hand. Kensaku, in *Journey Through Dark Night*, presumably Shiga himself, is finally unable to control himself and sadly makes his way to the brothels of Yoshiwara.

In Shiga's mood of confrontation with his father it was natural that he should have chosen as subject matter for "Otsu Junkichi," his story of 1912, the affair with the maid of several years earlier, one of the high points of that confrontation. In such a story he was able to express without reserve both his antagonism and his flaming ambition. But he was honest enough to express also the opposite, as can be seen from the quotation above.

The publication of "Otsu Junkichi" was the occasion for still another altercation with his father, and this time the latter suggested that it might be better for both of them if Naoya took up separate residence. The latter readily agreed, thinking to get more writing done that way, and moved to an inn in another part of Tokyo. Contrary to expectation, however, he found still less time for his writing than before, since he had a regular stream of visitors, members of the family and friends. A couple of months later he moved to Onomichi, a town on the Inland Sea.

Surrounded by the beautiful scenery of Onomichi, Shiga set to work upon his most ambitious writing project to date, a novel to be entitled *Tokito Kensaku*, after its hero. It was to be, in his own words, "a heroic tale" with himself as the hero. It would recount the history of his relations with his father and serve as a vehicle of self-definition. But the struggle of the past few months had greatly weakened him in both body and spirit. The picture he presents of himself in the story "The Kidnapping," which has the most detailed account of his days in Onomichi, is that of a man on the verge of a nervous breakdown. For the first half month he worked at his desk every night from midnight to morning in a state of pleasurable excitement, as if he were in direct confrontation with everything. (It is interesting to note that the work accomplished in this attitude of confrontation, the work, that is, in which he seeks to define and assert self, was always done in such a state of excitement.) But then he ran down. Soon he could work for no more than fifteen minutes at a time and the sensation of excitement was gone. He made a tour of Shikoku and the islands of the Inland Sea. He also made several visits to Tokyo, but his condition did not improve.

On a visit to Tokyo in the summer of 1913, on the very day that he had completed the story "An Incident," which tells about a child being hit by a streetcar, he himself was hit and seriously injured. He was hospitalized for a month, after which he went to Kinosaki Hot Springs to convalesce. The accident and his reflections upon it during the period of convalescence at Kinosaki mark a turning point in his life and in his writing. His encounter with death greatly weakened his attitude of confrontation and moderated his restless urgings toward self-assertion. He found himself entering a new world of union and harmony with nature. The accident and its aftermath are described in the story "At Kinosaki."

When he had fully recovered, Shiga returned once more to Onomichi, but within a week he was forced to go back to Tokyo because of a bad ear infection. He stayed on for a short time in Tokyo and then in June of 1914 went to Matsue on the Japan Sea to try to complete his novel. He had promised Natsume Soseki to have it ready for serialization in the *Asahi News* after Soseki's own *Kokoro* was concluded.

At Matsue he lived a far more peaceful life than at Onomichi. He was on familiar terms with "insects and birds and fish and grass and sky and, finally, men."[3] Here it was that he had what seems to have been his profoundest experience of harmony with nature, when he climbed Mt. Daisen. It was so moving an experience that twenty years later he was able to incorporate it into the powerful climactic scene of *Journey Through Dark Night*.

Pleasant as he found the life at Matsue, he still could not complete his novel. Upon his return to Tokyo he visited Soseki and with great embarrassment informed him that he would not be able to keep his promise. Until Soseki's death several years later, this refusal remained a heavy psychological burden, making it still more difficult for him to write.

From Matsue Shiga moved to Kyoto. He had become fond of visiting temples and museums of ancient art while in Onomichi. (On his trips to and from Tokyo he would stop and visit Kyoto and Nara.) Now in Kyoto he was able to indulge this fondness to his heart's content. These ancient monuments also helped to calm his restlessness and lure him out of the world of self-assertion and confrontation and into a more peaceful world of beauty and harmony.

Thus it was that the first three years of Taisho marked the most significant transition in Shiga's life and work, the transition from a positive attitude of self-assertion and "direct confrontation with everything" to a negative sense of becoming absorbed in the harmony of nature.

One last event of great importance took place in this climactic period, his marriage in December of 1914 to a cousin of Mushakoji, a widow with one child. This time he did not attempt to get his father's consent, which made the latter still more displeased with him and occasioned still another clash between father and son. Naoya cut the last string that bound him to his family by renouncing his right of inheritance. This act must have taken considerable courage and self-confidence, since his father had become a man of great financial means. Now at last Shiga was completely on his own.

The *Sturm und Drang* of these three years of Shiga's life was the cloth out of which some of his finest stories were cut: "My Mother's Death and the Coming of My New Mother," "Otsu Junkichi," "The Just Ones," "Claudius's Journal," and "Seibei's Gourds" in 1912; "An Incident" and "Han's Crime" in 1913. Moreover, the events and experiences of this period provided material for many of his later stories and his one long novel, *Journey Through Dark Night*.

V   *Reconciliation with Father*

The young couple made their home in Kyoto, but even at this distance the shadow of Naoya's father's displeasure hung over their lives. Shiga writes:

We remained in Kyoto only a short time. My bad relations with my father seemed to trouble Sadako very much and she was on her way to a nervous breakdown. I thought it best to move to another place, and so we took a house in Kamakura, next door to Naokata's [Naoya's uncle], but this was still worse for her condition and after a week we moved to Mt. Akagi.[4]

From this it appears how close, after all, was the tie between father and son—that the knowledge of the former's displeasure could have affected both of them so greatly and acted as a kind of incubus during what ought to have been the most blissful months of their married life. Shiga must have chosen beautiful Mt. Atagi in the hopes that nature would once again come to his rescue.

By now World War I was in full stride but at Akagi "almost no one speaks of it. All people talk about are the animals or the birds or the insects or other such objects of nature."[5] As Shiga had hoped, their proximity to nature in all its beauty did indeed restore both him and his bride to health and peace of soul. The quiet melancholy that Shiga had begun to experience after his brush with death was further deepened here on this mountain. It is this feeling of quiet melancholy that informs the story "Bonfire," which was written five years later but with his experience at Akagi in mind. This is one of his finest nature pieces.

In October Shiga and his wife moved to Abiko in Chiba Prefecture. There Shiga attempted once again to complete *Tokito Kensaku*, but to no avail, nor was he able to write much of anything else as long as this remained uncompleted. He finally gave up writing altogether and this silence continued for three years. In the loneliness of the life at Abiko the old anguish returned and the conflict with his father continued to darken their days.

The darkness was relieved by the birth of a daughter in the summer of 1916. Shiga could hardly contain his joy at having become a father. But his joy was short-lived: fifty-six days after birth the child died.

In December of 1916 Mushakoji Saneatsu, Shiga's most intimate friend and fellow writer, moved out to Abiko. Not only did the proximity of his good friend serve to brighten his days, but the latter's encouragement made it possible for him to begin to write again, and he wrote several stories in rapid succession, among them "The Good-Natured Couple" and "At Kinosaki." The latter, an account of his experience at Kinosaki Hot Springs while convalescing after his accident, is one of the finest pieces he ever wrote. It had taken Shiga three and a half years to understand all the implications of his experience at Kinosaki and to be able to put them down on paper.

The days became still brighter with the birth of his second daughter in July of 1917. The quiet life of Shiga and his family grew more and more harmonious, and this harmony prepared him for reconciliation with his father. He even came to realize how much of the fault for the quarrel was on his side. Finally, with the help of his family in Tokyo, father and son achieved the reconciliation which both desired above everything. It was effected with great naturalness, to their mutual joy and relief. The reconciliation and the events immediately leading up to it are the subject matter of Shiga's long story "Reconciliation," written at great speed soon after the joyful day.

Thus came to an end the long conflict with his father which had kept him at a high pitch of nervous excitement all through his youth; which had been responsible, more than anything else, for his attitude of confrontation and his determination to assert self; and which had given strength to his decision to become a writer. With this reconciliation, the confrontation and the self-assertion and the nervous excitement all came to an end. With one exception, which we shall describe shortly, all drama disappeared from his life, and the only drama to be found in his later work derives almost solely from the recollection of past events. This reconciliation was the major step to the silence of his later years.

The remaining five years spent at Abiko were fruitful and for the most part peaceful. He wrote more stories and sketches, among them "The Apprentice's God," "Bonfire," "Day of Snow," "Manazuru," and the longer "A Certain Man and the Death of his Sister," still another account of his conflict with his father, but this time as seen through the more objective eyes of a fictitious younger brother. He put together and published three volumes of his stories and sketches, and he turned once again to his uncompleted novel, *Tokito Kensaku*. This time he reshaped it completely, and under the new title of *Journey Through Dark Night* published what was to constitute the first half of the completed novel. By now his reputation as a writer was well established.

During his days at Abiko he had a steady stream of visitors, whose visits he relished and to whom he was always a most genial and generous host. He continued to grow in his intimacy with nature and in his love of Eastern art. At his own expense he published an album of reproductions of pieces of Eastern art.

Tragedy struck again in 1919 when his first son died about a month after birth. The following year another daughter was born, and the next year his grandmother died. In the years that followed three more daughters and one son were born.

VI   *The Yamashina Affair*

In 1923 Shiga and his family moved back again to Kyoto and Shiga was able to become still more familiar with ancient Japanese art and the monuments of the past. Unfortunately, his writing hit another slump. Try as he would, he could get nothing down on paper. His life was too peaceful, he concluded—too lacking in stimulus.

Then there took place what was perhaps the last dramatic event of his life. Until then he seems to have been completely faithful to his wife, but now he became infatuated with a young waitress of a Gion teahouse and entered into an affair with her. He was naïve enough to think that since he was still in love with his wife, it did not matter; that secure in the knowledge of his love, she could not very well object. He was unprepared for the violent domestic storm that followed upon discovery. Her vehement emotional reaction caused a moral crisis in Shiga. He had built his entire life upon the moral principle of "living sincerely," of being faithful to self, thinking that that was all that mattered. In the affair he was not conscious of having violated this principle. Yet here was violent repudiation of what he had done: his principle was powerless in the face of his wife's emotion.

Shiga had expected the affair to act as a stimulus in his settled life, and so it did for a time. In the excitement it generated he was able to turn out a series of stories centered on the affair. It even gave him the energy to bring *Journey Through Dark Night* well along the way to conclusion. But the stimulus was short-lived. After this first creative spurt he fell into complete silence, a silence punctuated only by the writing of a few sketches and of the final section of *Journey Through Dark Night* nine years later. After the war he began to write again, but these later pieces are mostly nature sketches and reminiscences. There were other reasons for this descent into silence, but these will be treated in Chapter 6.

CHAPTER 2

Japanese Naturalism
and the Shirakaba Writers

I *Japanese Naturalism*

S HIGA Naoya did not begin to write in a vacuum. He started out
as a member of a particular school of writing, the Shirakaba
(White Birch), with a definite theory of literature. Though Shiga
was always something of a maverick and not as representative of
Shirakaba as, for example, Mushakoji, he did share with other
members of the group certain philosophical and literary presup-
postions that gave a determinate character to his writing. Many
elements of his work that a reader unaware of this background
might take to be uniquely his own turn out upon investigation to
have been common to all of these writers.

The Shirakaba writers, in turn, did not invent the greater part of
their literary theory, but accepted it as axiomatic from their
predecessors, especially from the Naturalistic writers they sought to
supplant. For this reason it is necessary to give a brief survey of the
literary scene shortly prior to, and at the time of, Shiga's emergence
as a writer.

In his short introduction to Japanese literature (entitled *Japanese
Literature*), Donald Keene notes that the great problem for the
modern Japanese writer seeking to enter into the stream of world
literature was the lack of a tradition of individualism. "In the long
centuries between Lady Murasaki's day and the late nineteenth
century there is seldom a voice that speaks . . . with a truly personal note."[1] Therefore the great task for the modern writer in
assimilating Western realism was the creation of individuality. It
was this task that the Naturalists, and later the writers of Shirakaba,
attempted to perform.

The novelty of the Naturalistic movement in modern Japanese literature can readily be perceived if we take a look at the prevailing school of writers that preceded it, the Kenyusha. The writing of the Kenyusha people has been called "Japanese literature in Western dress." While borrowing Western techniques of realism, these writers wrote novels which differed very little in essence from the writings of feudal Japan. Of Ozaki Koyo, the chief representative of the Kenyusha school, Nakamura Mitsuo writes:

The views of individual and social life implied in his novels do not reflect the spirit of the times, nor do they show any sign of struggle with the problems of life. They depict a practical world in which every human activity can be explained in terms of pecuniary and sexual desires (lust and greed), and in which stereotyped handsome men and beautiful women, good and bad, rich and poor, etc. struggle for existence.[2]

From the first, Japanese Naturalism was very different from its European counterpart and model. The basic reason for this divergence is to be found in the differing implications of the word "scientific." For Zola and his followers it meant a revolt against the "unscientific" excesses of Romantic individualism, while for the Japanese Naturalists it meant rather a revolt against Japan's feudal past, especially against the traditional, formalized conventions dictating human behavior and restricting the natural development of the individual. It was a revolt, therefore, against traditional morality, traditional religion, traditional politics, traditional literature—in short, traditional institutions of all kinds. The Japanese Naturalist writers sought to "free man from his manifold illusions, empty logic, and hollow formulae for living; free him from the many idols and falsehoods he served."[3]

From the beginning, then, the movement was Romantic in terms of its goals. It very shortly became Romantic also in content. The first Naturalists, men such as Kosugi Tengai and Nagai Kafu, did not divorce man from his social background but merely sought to dissect him without reference to any standard, moral or aesthetic. But after the publication of Tayama Katai's novel *Futon* (Bedding), the Naturalistic novel became so completely autobiographical that nothing but the writer's individual self found expression in it. Under the cloak of Naturalism there developed a mode completely antithetical to the Naturalism that was known and practiced in Europe.

In 1906 was published the first great Japanese Naturalistic novel, Shimazaki Toson's *Hakai* (The Broken Commandment), telling the story of a young man of an outcast class and the problems he encounters in keeping hidden the secret of his origins. The novel had as its background the problem of the *eta* class and showed a real concern for social questions. But at the same time Toson poured himself so completely into his hero, Ushimatsu, that the latter became an expression of the author's own self. Toson, by confessing the innermost secrets of his heart through the persona of Ushimatsu, succeeded in creating a living character with considerable psychological depth. The other characters, however, were seen only from the outside. Thus, *Hakai* was both Japan's first real problem novel, criticizing society after the manner of the European Naturalists, and the first step in the direction of the autobiographical novel.

A year later Tayama Katai published *Futon*, which told the story of Katai's own love affair in middle age with a young lady staying with him and his family. Though he modeled this work on a novel by Hauptmann, *Lonely Lives*, Katai chose to imitate the hero of the novel rather than the novelist: that is to say, he identified himself so closely with his main character that all distance between them was erased and the novel became a monologue presenting the subjective perceptions of the author.

While Toson had struggled to express his inner world through the structure of fiction, Katai rejected fiction and confessed the reality of his own life as it actually was. It was this novel that set the form for those to follow. Thus, the writer Kume Masao at the end of the Taisho period was able to say: "I take the autobiographical novel to be, in the strictest sense of the word, the foundation, the mainstream, the essence of literature—or, if the term 'literature' seems too broad, at least of prose composition."[4] Nakamura's comment on this statement is that over half of the best novels of the Taisho period (1912—26), regardless of the literary school to which the writer belonged, followed the style of *Futon* and were written as if in further development of it.[5] In another passage Nakamura goes still further and claims that the autobiographical-novel form as established by Katai became the standard form for the modern

Japanese novel as a whole and the foundation for the concept of prose literature held by Japanese writers even into the postwar period.[6]

When presented with the two models for a future literature, *Hakai* and *Futon*, why did the writers, including Toson himself (in his later work) choose the latter in preference to the former? Nakamura gives several reasons for this. One is that by having the writer himself become the novel's principal character and live out the theme of the novel, the writer could imitate Western literature with something more than merely external imitation, such as that of the Kenyusha writers.

In such a performance it was necessary for the novelist to take upon himself and live out the general mood and problems of the hero of the foreign novel he chose to imitate, somthing which was impossible for the writers of the previous age, steeped as they were in feudal morality and the peculiar atmosphere of the literature that derived from the Edo period.

For the novelist to give himself entirely to this exercise of imaginative identification was for him to establish himself as a representative of the new age. It gave the novelist also a further advantage. By depicting in a Japanese context a hero with the sensibility of the hero of a foreign novel, the view of life of a particular foreign writer, it was thought, could be transplanted in Japan, alive, unadulterated, full-bodied. Thus, if the novelist took as his hero a character from a tale of Poe, this in itself constituted the adaptation of Poe to Japan; and the same if he took a hero from a Tolstoy novel.[7]

A second reason for the rapid and universal acceptance of the autobiographical as the standard form for the novel was that this mode seemed best suited for the revolt against tradition and for the liberation of the individual. There was a general outcry against all illusion, and this, for some reason hard to understand, included also literary illusion, or the element of fiction in literature. The Naturalistic critic Hasegawa Tenkei, in 1906 in a magazine article entitled "Art in an Age That Rejects All Illusion," wrote:

The art of the future must be an art that rejects all the frivolous elements of an art born in an age that was under the strong influence of all kinds of illusions. It must be an art that establishes truth *(shinjitsu)* itself as its foundation. In this age that is bent upon throwing over all illusions, what everyone desires is an unadorned art that depicts the truth. Painting, sculpture, the novel, the drama—all must progress in this direction.[8]

To Tenkei and the other Naturalists fiction and polished style were "frivolous elements," illusions to be dispensed with. To believe in a world and in characters that have been constructed through the power of the writer's imagination is equivalent to believing in religious myth, something possible only in an age of superstition and ignorance, but totally unsuited to an age that has thrown over its illusions. In a day when the only truth that is recognized is scientific truth and when all previous illusions have been shattered against the firm wall of science, literature must utilize a realism born in a climate of science and stand firmly upon fact. Only what the writer himself has seen, heard, and felt is to be depicted. All else is but the fabricated Romanticism of the past and has lost the power to stir men's hearts.

Thus, while Zola, whom the Japanese Naturalists thought they were following, strove to depict reality in all of its social dimensions and in terms of the problems of the age, the Japanese Naturalists placed primary emphasis upon the individual's experience of life. In the West, Naturalistic literature was an anti-individualistic literature born as a reaction to the excessive individualism of the Romantics; in Japan, it was a literature that overexaggerated the individuality of the writer, and thus was a certain kind of Romanticism.

Under Katai and his followers the autobiographical novel became the medium through which the writer, with as little intervention of form as possible, presented his individual "heart" in a direct appeal to the reader. This kind of novel was defined as "a novel in which the writer himself appears in his work to make his direct pronouncements on life—or more exactly, in which the writer making his direct pronouncements on life has become the novel. It is a novel in which the predominating consciousness is not of what is written but of who is writing."[9]

The Naturalists rejected all the ideals of a former age and sought to forge a new morality based upon the one principle of fidelity to self. The truth they pursued was the truth of self; the principal virtue they extolled was "sincerity," a synonym for fidelity to self. "Renounce empty lies, eschew all decoration, scrutinize the self, and make earnest confession of what you find," wrote Shimamura Hogetsu.[10] The writers' lives were the proving grounds for this new morality, and their works a kind of progress report on their "asceticism." This was another reason for rejecting the element of fiction: if lies were incorporated into the text of their "proof," their purpose could never be realized.

The search for a new morality in the writer's individual self was possible because this self was also nature; and every trifling event of everyday life was meaningful, therefore, as a manifestation of nature. Katai puts it succinctly as follows: "My inner life is also a Nature. Just as the rest of the universe is Nature, so I myself am also Nature."[11] Since he sees himself as representative of nature, the effort to establish any more universal view of man is unnecessary labor; there is no need to reach out to others or to society in general.

Katai goes one step further. When self lives according to its nature, he believed, the distinction between self and other disappears: "What is natural, what is true, what is close to the laws of things, what is most in rhythm—this is Self, and at the same time it is Other. Accordingly, whatever is natural will resonate most clearly with Other. Here is to be found the life and root of art."[12] Thus, the writer believed that in living according to his nature and depicting himself without varnish he was choosing the very best way for educing a response in others. Katai urges that the writer reject all intellectual presuppositions and judgments and follow his own nature. If he does this, his "subjective" will become "objective."

Such a theory of art could not but have far-reaching consequences with regard to the writing, the writer, and the reading public. First, with regard to the kind of novel it produced, the autobiographical novel had only the one character, the "I"; all the other characters were filtered through the one consciousness and received their value from it. A fortiori, society and social problems were totally alien to it. Moreover, even the "I" character itself tended to be an abstraction, since thoughts, feelings, and actions were presented as a series of impressions without interpretation or analysis, or even an attempt at consistency, and without reference to a standard, since they themselves constituted the standard. For adequate communication the reader's knowledge of the writer, supplying necessary background and detail, had to be presupposed. Further, the central character was almost always a writer, or at least an artist, since the novelist could never range far from the "truth" of his own life.

With regard to the novelist, the writer of the autobiographical novel was isolated from society and felt no responsibility toward it. For all his protestations, he was no more in tune with the age than his predecessors, the Kenyusha writers, had been. Moreover, he soon ran out of material and found it necessary to conduct his real life in such a way that it would provide matter for his novels, often with disastrous effect.

Finally, with regard to the reading public, the autobiographical novel by reason of its narrow and repetitive nature could not long retain a large circle of readers. The writer eventually wound up writing only for other writers. Another reason for this in the case of the Naturalistic autobiographical novel was the depressing tone of most of the writing. The Naturalistic novelist depicted the pain and boredom of everyday life, unrelieved by any ray of idealism or hope.

II *The Shirakaba Writers*

We have already seen that Shiga Naoya in 1910 at the age of twenty-seven joined with other graduates of Gakushuin to start the magazine *Shirakaba*. None of these writers were yet known when they began writing, but through their work in this magazine several, especially Shiga, Mushakoji Saneatsu, Arishima Takeo, Arishima Ikuma, and Satomi Ton, soon became very famous. Weary of the gloomy pessimism of the Naturalistic writers, readers turned with relief to the optimistic idealism of these young Shirakaba aristocrats, and continued to support the magazine until it stopped publication in 1923, after the great Tokyo earthquake.

From the very first issue *Shirakaba* was not merely a literary publication, but an art magazine in the broadest sense of the word. Not only did it introduce its readers to Tolstoy, Whitman, Strindberg, Maeterlinck, Ibsen, Rolland, and other European and American writers, but it encouraged appreciation of Western art and sculpture. Van Gogh, the French Impressionists, Cézanne, and Rodin were among the artists taken up in its pages. By attempting to familiarize their readers with the thought, culture, and life of contemporary Europe, the Shirakaba writers felt that they were helping Japan break out of its old cast and that they themselves

were becoming "children of the world," their own phrase. Thus for
them the literature and art they introduced was more than a model
for imitation; it was, rather, spiritual sustenance contributing to a
more universal humanity. They went from art to universal humanity without the intervention of human society.

Society as such had little place in their theory. Their central ideal
was that of the infinite potentiality of the individual self. Human
happiness lay in the realization of this potential. Therefore man's
only moral imperative was to develop and remain faithful to the
self—to make much of the self, never to lose sight of it, never to be
betrayed into expression or action that was false to it. This very
fidelity to self, they believed, was the best way, indeed the only
way, of making a contribution to society. To advance the self was
automatically to advance others. To act in the best interests of self
was to act in the best interests of society, in the best interests of
mankind. The lighthouse keeper has no right to give to the poor the
oil he needs to keep his light burning. But men are all lighthouse
keepers and must make certain first of all that they themselves
shine. Only then can they, through their light, be of service to
others.

In the conduct of their daily lives the Shirakaba writers were not
motivated by abstract ideals of duty and responsibility or of concrete goals to be achieved; they depended entirely on "felt
realizations" (*jikkan*, a word not easy to translate into English).
They were motivated, in short, to do what "felt right" to them.
That is why the hero of Shiga's *Journey Through Dark Night* can
say that for him good and evil are the same as like and dislike.

The reason why they could be so certain that the interests of self
were also the interests of society and mankind in general was that
they posited a kind of Emersonian world soul or universal will that
flowed directly into all individual selves, so that the high tide of
one's self automatically overflowed to nourish the selves of others.
They thought that this will of the universe willed man's happiness,
and so they believed in human progress. Man's highest and most
worthy aim and that most conducive to progress was to unite his
will completely with the universal will. This transcendental power
they believed in was not conceived of as a personal God, and their
"religion" was something highly abstract and syncretic, admitting
of no distinction between God, Buddha, or Christ. They believed

not so much in religion as in believing in religion.

Shirakaba literature is sometimes presented as the antithesis of Naturalism. In reality, as can be concluded from the above discussion, the two schools of writing had much in common. In the first place, they both looked to the self as the proper arena for the discovery of truth. Self, for both, was the nature to be explored and expressed. The Shirakaba writers, no less then the Naturalist, accepted the autobiographical mode as the ideal form of prose writing and sought to dispense as much as possible with the element of fiction. For all their protestations of interest in society and human progress, they, too, like the Naturalists, were locked in the individual self and closed to the world outside them; like the Naturalists they sought to expose their "hearts" straightforwardly and expected the reader to "resonate" with them.

They differed from the Naturalists in two main points. First, whereas the Naturalists looked into themselves and found only gloom, sickness, and desperation, unrelieved by any ideal, the Shirakaba writers—though their actual condition was often dark enough, witness the world of the first part of Shiga's *Journey Through Dark Night*—could look to the universal will guaranteeing their eventual happiness and that of the human race. But that they could continue to hold on to this optimism was due less to the strength of their philosophical convictions than to the actual circumstances of their lives, and this is the second point of difference. All the young men of Shirakaba were of aristocratic or at least of wealthy family. They had not to trouble themselves about making a living and could devote their lives to "art" without being concerned about their productiveness. They were all *botchan*, the Japanese term, largely pejorative, for young men well circumstanced and not having to worry about making their way in the world.

These first two chapters have concerned themselves with Shiga Naoya's life and with the stream of literature into which he entered when he decided to join in the Shirakaba venture. The one will illuminate many of the elements to be found in his work, since so much of that work is either directly or indirectly autobiographical. The other will explain why he wrote in the form he did and will make it easier to appreciate the greatness of some of his stories. Though he was hampered by an impossible theory of prose fiction, he did at times accomplish the very most that could be accomplished in such a defective genre as the autobiographical novel; and in several of his works—admittedly all too few—he broke out of the genre completely to write some of the finest short stories in the Japanese language. It is only after examining his handicaps that we are in a position to evaluate his achievement.

CHAPTER 3

Mine What Is in Me

"I must spend my life in bringing out what is in me. I must mine what is in me," Shiga wrote in his journal on March 8, 1912. He had already been doing this since his first published sketch, "One Morning," in 1908, and he continued to do so to the very end. Almost all of his writings are closely linked to the events and moods of the various periods of his life. In this chapter we shall consider his more directly autobiographical sketches and stories, viewing them chronologically in the light of the events and states of mind they reflect. In Chapter 4 we shall consider *Journey Through Dark Night,* which is still another recapitulation of the period of his life from 1912 to 1917. Occasionally Shiga was able to transcend the autobiographical mode and find objective fictional symbols to express his inner states. These stories—among the very best that he wrote—will be taken up in Chapter 5.

I "One Morning" (1908)

In a commentary on his work written in 1928, Shiga had this to say about his first published piece, "One Morning":

I wrote "One Morning" in the afternoon of January 13 (1908), the day of the memorial service commemorating the third anniversary of my grandfather's death. It describes an event that took place that same morning. I was twenty-five. I suppose I could call it my maiden work. I had been trying for some time to put a story together, but nothing would fall into shape. I would have a plot in mind, but when I got it down on paper, it did not come out as I wished. If I tried to write the story in one sitting, the result was a rough piece—all bones; and if I took my time at it, my pen ran off in pursuit of every small detail until the general outline was lost. But with "One Morning" it was different. The story has a very simple content, and I found it unexpectedly easy to write. After I had finished it, I felt that I had finally succeeded in writing a short story. Since I was twenty-five years old, this was—it seems to me from my present point of view—already late. From experience such as this, I gradually learned how to write. (X,170)

The action of the story begins the previous night when Shintaro's grandmother tries to get him to go to bed at a reasonable hour, so that he will be able to get up in time to prepare for the memorial service. Paying scant attention to her words, he does not turn out his light and go to sleep until after one. The following morning she comes to call him at a little after six. Three times she calls and each time he mumbles that he is getting up, but doesn't. Finally she shouts at him and he gets angry. They have an exchange of words, and he remains in bed, now to spite her. She makes a show of folding up the bedding and putting it away in the closet, thinking that he will take pity on her age and come to her assistance. Instead he watches her coldly. Finally she gets angry and calls him an ingrate. He answers her so maliciously that she leaves the room in rage and tears. When he realizes she will not be back to call him again, he finally feels like getting up. He rises and gets dressed. He decides he will go to Suwa to ice-skate the following day. Three students fell through the ice and drowned there recently, so that ought to make his grandmother worry about him. At this point she enters the room again and in an obvious attempt at reconciliation consults him about the writing brush to be used for the memorial service. Shintaro answers sullenly at first, but gradually warms up to her. He decides to call off his excursion and, smiling now, puts the rest of the bedding away. His eyes mist over with tears and soon he is crying so hard that he cannot see. When the tears finally stop, he feels extremely refreshed and goes to watch his brother and sisters at play in the next room.

The piece is hardly more than a sketch, filling no more than five pages in the standard edition of Shiga's works. Shiga himself refers to it as a "nonstory" in the journal entry for the day on which he wrote it. It was only later that he came to regard it as his "first story."

But for all its narrow compass, this little piece serves as a fine introduction to the much-lauded Shiga style. Every word is in its proper place, carrying its proper burden. The impression is given that no word is superfluous and no word should be added. In several brief sentences are narrated the events of the previous night, which set the scene for the quarrel of the morning. The account of the quarrel itself is succinct, given mostly through dialogue. The words are chosen so sensitively that they record every slight nuance and fluctuation of tone from the casual beginning, through the heated climax, to the serene denouement.

There are few adjectives. Emotional attitudes are presented indirectly, sometimes through skillful use of dialogue, sometimes through other means. For example, nothing could better show Shintaro's feeling of childish pique at the height of the quarrel than his decision to go skating in order to have his grandmother worry about his safety; and the concluding scene with his brother and sisters at their play conveys well the feeling of relief and refreshment after reconciliation has been achieved. Even when Shintaro, after the reconciliation, begins to cry so hard that he cannot see to put the bedding away, the writing is not sentimental but under strict control.

The style of "One Morning," then, is splendid; but the contents cannot be considered other than trivial, especially when the reader reflects that Shintaro is not a little boy, as his actions and words would seem to indicate, but a grown man of twenty-five. It is impossible to agree with the Japanese critic who gives this piece fulsome praise for its depiction of an intense experience in the life of a man who "lives with great sincerity and great intensity, and in whom feeling and action are perfectly joined."[1] The same critic points out that the events depicted are not recollected in tranquillity, but are so intensely relived that the details of the writing select themselves, a fact which accounts for the power of the style. A number of critics place a high value on this piece for the intensity of life, of self-realization, of "sincerity" to be found in it. They see value too in the way Shintaro entrusts himself entirely to nature and its processes. They point out that already in the movement of this little piece is to be discerned the pattern of the movement of much of Shiga's work: from confrontation to head-on collision to reconciliation, always following the way of nature. All this may be true to a point, but it is hard to see what value can be assigned to a "self-realization" and a "sincerity" that is so little distinguishable from immature self-centeredness and, indeed, childish tantrum. This is a problem, however, that we will have with most of Shiga's "self-realization" pieces. Here in the consideration of Shiga's first "story"

Japanese and non-Japanese critical evaluation may already part ways.

II "For Grandmother" (1911)

"For Grandmother" was written almost four years after "One Morning," but it can be looked upon as a companion piece to it. It gives the reader a much better understanding of the deep love there was between grandmother and grandson, and the great concern each had for the other's well-being. In fact, "One Morning" takes on a richer meaning when it is read in the light of the later story.

The story begins:

> I often feel that all my friends have antipathy toward me. Though I know this feeling is not healthy and only transitory, still when I go to visit anyone, I feel as if I were under attack and I begin to say and do boorish things. When I am by myself again, I am always filled with anger and unbearable loneliness. At such times my grandmother comes to mind. "After all, she's the only person I can rely on." (I, 244)

Five years earlier when his grandfather was dying, his grandmother was at the sick man's side nursing him day and night. Despite his own love for his grandfather, he was afraid that if she continued at this pace she would follow her husband to the grave. Then when his grandfather died, an albino mortician was immediately upon the scene to ask to have the funeral. The grandson was both astounded and disgusted at this "rapid service." The albino made such an unpleasant impression that he was unable to forget him for a long time thereafter.

Two years later his grandmother fell ill, partly as a result of the trouble he himself was causing in the family. He was filled with worry and fear that she too might die. This grandmother, who had raised him from childhood, was a woman of strong character, and he had often had highly emotional exchanges with her, but these had served rather to strengthen the already firm bond between them. He grew more and more concerned about her health. Then one night he had a dream in which the albino mortician appeared as the harbinger of death. From that time he felt he had to do something to protect his grandmother from this man. Perhaps his hatred for the mortician began to have its effect, because his grandmother gradually regained her health, and the albino, who until then had often been seen in the neighborhood, suddenly disappeared from view. He believed that he had somehow caused the man's death and he rejoiced over this, and even more over his grandmother's complete recovery.

Unlike "One Morning," "For Grandmother" has both the organic unity and the scope of development—plot, characterization, atmosphere, and theme—that we usually associate with the genre of short story. The principal unifying element binding together the diversified incidents is the albino mortician. He first appears at the time of the grandfather's death as a kind of symbol of death, and his disappearance at the end symbolizes the triumph of life. The theme is, of course, the love of grandmother and grandson. It is her concern for him that is one of the main causes of her illness, and it is his concern for her that occasions the fantasies concerning the albino.

The characters of both Shiga and his grandmother and the nature of their relationship are so much better developed here than in "One Morning" that the immaturity of the grandson does not pose the problem that it did in the earlier sketch. The two are first seen at the bedside of the dying grandfather. She has been at her husband's side since she was sixteen and her deep love for him is evident in the frenetic energy with which she nurses him round the clock. The grandson is filled with grief as he watches his beloved grandfather approach death. At the same time he fears that his still more beloved grandmother will burn herself out and follow him to the grave. When the old man finally dies, his fears seem to have been justified since his grandmother acts for a time as one who has no longer any function in the world.

As in "One Morning," the grandmother is indulgent and the grandson is spoiled. Here too he grumbles when she tries to get him out of bed in the morning, and they quarrel. They quarrel also about many other things. After one such exchange she follows him into the bathroom, where he is taking his bath, and whacks him on his bare back with a switch. He shouts, "You can't hurt me!" and she hits him all the harder, then leaves the room, slamming the door behind her. Yet it is with obvious affection that the grandson recalls the incident. And later when she is ill and becomes difficult for the other members of the family to manage, it is the grandson that takes over and scolds her into submission. In passages such as the following the deep love that binds the two is clearly seen:

Even before I lost my mother when I was thirteen, I had been raised almost single-handedly by my grandmother. Both the immediate members of my family and more distant relatives attributed my shiftlessness and selfish character to my grandmother's blind love. When I was alone with her in her sickroom, she often spoke of this and cried, and I in turn would either cry or get angry. My tears would flow especially at the mention of my dead mother, and I would imagine the day when my grandmother too would be dead, and I would be completely alone in the world. (I, 247)

But more than anything else, it is the symbol of the albino mortician that suggests the depth of the hero's relationship with both grandparents. The albino's appearance immediately after the grandfather's death, like a maggot that has been waiting to feast on flesh, objectifies the horror the grandson feels at the departure from this life of the man he loved so much and sought all his life to emulate. From that moment the albino becomes gradually the very incarnation of death and evil.

Two years later at the height of the hero's conflict with his father, his grandmother falls gravely ill and he fears that she will die. She is finally able to get up from her sickbed, but she is still very weak and before long falls desperately ill again. The grandson has a sur-realistic dream in which he sees the albino stealing quietly through the house, which he has placed under a kind of curse. After this dream, the mortician becomes still more hateful to him. His appearance on the street reminds him of "a wild beast, starved and stalking his prey." He fancies that if he wishes his grandmother to live until he is at least forty, he must do something about the albino's curse, but he doesn't know what he should do.

The grandmother grows still worse, and the grandson, now almost in a frenzy, watches over her as she lies on her sickbed, struggling for her breath. As her struggle becomes more and more desperate, he fancies that he sees in the corner of the dark room the glow of the albino's ash-colored eyes, and he concentrates all his strength on staring them down, as if his grandmother's recovery depended upon it. When the grandmother does finally get well, the grandson reflects: "The first illness and the second one, too, she had been at the point of death, but somehow managed to recover. . . . If I hadn't been home, she would not now be alive. I had power over the albino, or whatever it was that came to assault her" (I, 252). Somehow he is not able to question the truth of this.

This story shows the state of Shiga's nerves at the time of its writing (1911). He himself calls it morbid. "It will probably seem morbid and extremely fantastic," he writes, "but for me at that time it was a record of fact, not a bit darker than the reality. Now I realize that I myself was morbid when I wrote it"(X, 172).

The morbid condition of the hero is a reflection of Shiga's own condition in the year before he left home. In such a condition, nightmarish fantasy tends to become indistinguishable from reality. This can be seen even more clearly in "Confused Head," written a year earlier.

III   "Confused Head" (1910)

Tsuda Kiyomatsu is a young man aspiring to be a writer. His seven years of life as a Christian (from his seventeenth year to his twenty-fourth) come to an end when he is unable to reconcile the Christian teaching on chastity with his own strong sexual desires. Unable to break himself of his habit of self-abuse and assured by the minister of his church that sins against chastity are every bit as grave as murder, he concludes, after great agony of conscience, that he is a moral cripple cursed with more than normal sexual appetite. His state of mind alternates between anguished contrition for his failings and bitter resentment toward the minister and toward Christianity itself.

His problem becomes all the more acute when a young widow, O-Natsu, a relative of his mother's, comes to live in the Tsuda home. Though he instinctively dislikes her, she is educated and can discuss literature, particularly novels, with him, and so he spends much time talking with her.

One night he reads to her from the novel he is writing, a novel that gives expression to his pent-up sexual longings. As he reads, both become aroused and Tsuda has his first experience of the other sex. As a result, the conflict within him grows to alarming proportions. He has the great joy of having touched upon eternal mystery, of having eaten from the tree of knowledge. But greater still are his pangs of conscience at having committed sin. In the days that follow he continues to find O-Natsu repulsive, but is unable to stay away from her, and their relationship continues, undiscovered by the other members of the family. He sees that he is a weak man, without a self, who can neither believe nor positively reject belief, nor remain content to do neither. He feels himself to be without religion, without morality, without society, and without family. As a result, he falls into a state of complete despair. With the inconsistency that has come to mark his thoughts and actions, he thinks with pleasure of O-Natsu's dying, but then impulsively elopes with her.

Living on O-Natsu's savings, the two go from one resort inn to another. His head becomes as confused as his heart, and he gradually loses his ability to distinguish between reality and dream. One part of himself hates O-Natsu and wishes her dead, but another part is in love with her. She has become as necessary to him as liquor to the alcoholic.

One night when his head is more confused than usual, O-Natsu playfully throws herself upon him, and he has the illusion that he is about to be killed. Unable to throw her off, he strikes her, giving her a bloody nose. After this incident, she treats him as a stranger. He tries to win her back, realizing that she is all that stands between him and nonexistence. But he is unsuccessful and the two grow to hate each other more and more as their minds become more and more confused.

One night after watching a worker skillfully insert his needles into a straw mat he is making, Tsuda drives one of the needles through O-Natsu's throat. He loses consciousness of things around him for several hours and comes to himself at an inn some distance from the scene of the crime. He tries to make his escape but loses consciousness again. He awakens to find himself this time in a prison for the insane. Two years later he is free and recounting this story to a man at the inn at which he is staying.

"Confused Head" reads like the account of a nightmare that has been somewhat retouched for the telling, and indeed Shiga does state that " 'Confused Head' was written out of my experience at a time when I was on the point of a nervous breakdown and is based on a hint I received in a dream" (X, 171).

Though certain passages are concrete and graphic enough, the story has the overall fuzziness and lack of motivation associated with the world of dream. The characters are seen through a kind of haze and never really come alive. Tsuda, already well along the way to degeneration when the story begins, is a monster with no redeeming touches of humanity. The reader is never given any insight into the more human person he may once have been or any reason to hope that he will ever be other than he is. He is absolutely without will, the total victim of impulse. He cannot be held to account for his actions, but by the same token his actions have no more significance than those of a madman, which indeed he finally becomes.

The story does have some interest by reason of its autobiographical elements. Tsuda's problems with chastity, his break with Christianity, his progressively deepening mood of frustration and despair—these were all experienced to some degree by Shiga himself. But this is all much better told in three later stories, "Otsu Junkichi," "Reconciliation," and "A Certain Man and the Death of His Sister," and in *Journey Through Dark Night.* As might be expected, Shiga's fine style, which makes so much of concreteness and selection of detail, is not much in evidence here.

IV   "Otsu Junkichi" (1912)

We saw in the introductory chapter that Shiga in 1907, at the age of twenty-five, made up his mind to marry a girl from the country who was serving the family as a maid. We saw also that this marriage was vigorously opposed by his father and grandmother. The "romance," if such it could be called, dragged on for several months and then fizzled out. Shiga's relations with his father became much worse as a result of this affair and continued thereafter to deteriorate.

"Otsu Junkichi" was written five years after the event. The story has two parts. Part I begins very much as "Confused Head" did, with an account of Junkichi's difficulty in obeying the Christian rule of chastity. The rest of Part I and the first half of Part II tell of his relations with a young girl of mixed blood. The central incident is a dance party at which Junkichi is ill at ease and made to feel his lack of social grace. He does not know how to dance and he is awkward in conversation, especially with women. Some time after the party he exchanges photographs with the girl (one of the first steps in arranging a marriage), but since in the interim she has put on weight, she no longer conforms to his image of the ideal woman and he loses all interest in her.

From the middle of Part II it is his love affair with Chiyo, the maid, that is central. Without preparation or even previous mention of the girl, Junkichi suddenly announces that he gradually fell in love with her. What follows is surely one of the strangest love affairs in all of literature. At first he is reluctant to tell her of his love. His reluctance, he realizes, stems from the recognition that she is not beautiful and will not be an asset in his life and work. It stems, in short, from his personal vanity.

Still he cannot put her out of his mind. He calls her to his room and tells her that he loves her, but not with so very passionate a love. He sounds her out to see if she would marry him if he proposed to her. In the course of the conversation he becomes disgusted with his own cunning, and, perhaps in reaction to this, impulsively places his mother's ring on her finger and proposes marriage to her. She goes into a faint. As she lies on the floor of his room, he is repelled at the sight of her sweaty neck covered with downy hair and even wonders if her faint is not a stratagem to prevent him from going further with her. He stands for a long time staring down at her as from a distance. This is hardly the stance of a lover whose beloved has just agreed to marriage.

Junkichi and Chiyo come together secretly as man and wife. The family will not hear of their marriage and threaten to send Chiyo home. Junkichi defends her, but even now he is so far from being the blind lover that he can tell a friend that his love is not the least impassioned and that he is troubled at times with doubts about it.

All through the story Junkichi has avoided a direct meeting with his father, but finally he sees that such a meeting is inevitable. He goes to his father's room at midnight when he is already in bed. Naturally his father refuses to talk to him then, or the next day, since he must leave the house early. Junkichi returns to his room in a rage and begins throwing things around, making enough noise to awaken everyone in the house. The story ends with him pouring out his troubles in a letter to a friend in Paris.

Shiga undoubtedly had material here for a short story, but he did not shape and order it. The only principle of organization is the chronological sequence of Junkichi's feelings and actions. Moreover, Shiga identifies himself too completely with his hero to allow for the objectivity required in fiction.

Even taken as autobiography the work is defective. Junkichi is not sufficiently interesting a character to justify so minute an observation of him. At twenty-five he acts more like an adolescent of fifteen. The spoiled brat of a wealthy family who has always had his own way and everything he wanted, he has few if any winning qualities (except perhaps his frankness in self-exposure). He himself recognizes this fact. In a passage in Part I he says that he had decided to become a writer, but had no confidence that he would be able to make a living at writing. So he will become a teacher of English in a country middle-school and write in his spare time. His father, he reports, thinks that he is stubborn, proud, hot-headed, a cry baby, unable to stand on his own two feet, lazy, and perhaps even a socialist. Later his grandmother adds to this litany: "Your father and all the relatives are always telling me that it's because I've spoiled you that you have become such a good-for-nothing. . . . You sleep till after noon every day, and don't go to classes. All you're good for is visiting with friends and going to plays and music halls" (VI, 39). He recognizes too that despite his great ambition to become a writer, all that has come from his pen so far has been a "thin shrill sound" that has not traveled beyond the circle of his friends. But he resolves that this will change.

The story as a whole is dull reading. There are, however, one or two scenes that come to life. In these scenes we find again Shiga's sharp eye for detail and his great impressionability. The dance party in Part I, for example, especially Junkichi's awkwardness in such a social situation, is well drawn. Another scene that comes alive is that of Junkichi's quarrel with his grandmother. Here find expression all the nuances of a very complicated relationship.

"Otsu Junkichi" was the story that won for Shiga his first public recognition as a writer, and also the first story for which he was paid. Its favorable reception was more than a little due to the motif of self-affirmation that it sounded, a motif that had a special appeal in an age that was painfully aware of the lack of self-expression in Japanese life and literature.

In a very discerning commentary on this story, Nakamura Mitsuo compares "Otsu Junkichi" with the earlier "Confused Head." Like Tsuda in the latter, Otsu too is without religion, morality, or family. He must build up from nothing his own system of values. But whereas the hero of "Confused Head" does a good bit of self-reflecting and analysis, Otsu does none whatsoever. He has perfect self-assurance with regard to the reasonablesness and accuracy of his own judgment and the correctness of his actions. Not unlike the inmates of an insane asylum, he develops a logic of his own, a logic that depends upon and flows from feeling and that has as its function the setting in order of impressions.

Nakamura goes on to state that "Otsu Junkichi" is a work commemorating the writer's success in rejecting Christianity and all religion. Here already Shiga begins to affirm a code of ethics that is based on personal feeling. Literature has become religion and fills the writer's need of something for the spirit. Instead of Uchimura Kanzo representing Christ for him, he himself becomes Christ and God.

The whole of "Otsu Junkichi" is a ceremony of self-deification conducted with solemn gestures by a dweller on a deserted island. Thus, Junkichi's strange behavior at the end. . . . is but the completion of the ritual. As in most of even the best autobiographical novels, neither the hero nor the writer is aware of the humor. . . . Junkichi's lack of consideration [for those who are asleep in the house] cannot be attributed to his youth or to his inborn nature. What is to be noted here is that this exaggerated self-worship has become his aesthetics, his moral code, and almost his religion.[2]

It is easier to agree with Nakamura than with Hirotsu Kazuo, who sees this self-centeredness redeemed by a heart that is essentially pure.

If there were not at the roots of Shiga's character an uncompromising purity of the heart ever turned toward the good, this pig-headed self-centeredness would have been a poison poisoning his entire character. But he does have this purity of heart. Thus, that which for some characters would be poison, is for Shiga rather a most treasured medicine strengthening his character.[3]

The hero's gestures of self-exaltation are, as Nakamura says, ridiculous, and the writer's lack of objective perspective make this story of less importance as a piece of literature than as a fragment of biography.

V   "The Kidnapping" (1914)

Like "Confused Head" and "For Grandmother," "The Kidnapping" is a strange combination of autobiography and nightmare. It begins as pure autobiography, an account of Shiga's circumstances and feelings during his stay at Onomichi and the days immediately preceding it, but gradually develops into most implausible fantasy, as the hero kidnaps a little girl and takes her to live with him in his small house overlooking the harbor.

The autobiographical action of the story is that of the period from October of 1912 to early 1913. The story itself was written in late 1913 and published in 1914. Between the two periods there took place one of the most significant events in Shiga's life, his accident in Tokyo and convalescence in Kinosaki. It was this experience, as we have already seen, that weakened his stance of "confrontation with all things" and set him on the road toward harmony and reconciliation. The Shiga that recounts the story, however, has still far to go before he grasps the full meaning of the Kinosaki experience. He has lost the power and the will to assert himself, and is still as desperately confused as ever.

The story begins with the following confrontation between father and son:

"Spending all your days like this, what in the world do you intend to make of your future?" my father asked me one morning, with contempt in his voice. "What have I done to merit having a lazy, good-for-nothing son like you?"

He went on to say that the very sight of me disgusted him. With someone like me around, how was it possible to raise the little ones properly? He spoke as if all the evils of the day had come together in me. With me around, the whole family deserved to be ostracized from society. His words were like a brutal slap in the face. I answered him with words equally harsh. Then I burst into tears, the first time I had done so in a long time. (II, 132)

The next day, although it is raining, the son piles all his belongings into a cart and moves to an inn in Kyobashi. He stays there for only half a month, then goes to live in Onomichi. In Onomichi he rents a little house halfway up a mountain, from which he has a view of the city, the sea, and the islands. He makes necessary repairs in the house and buys the furniture he will need.

This is his first experience of being completely on his own, free to do as he pleases. Three years earlier he had gone to Kyoto with the intention of staying there. He had taken all his possessions and had bade farewell to his friends. He had spent the first day in Kyoto looking for a place to live, but unsuccessful in finding a lodging to

his liking, he had become disgusted and had impulsively caught the
night train back to Tokyo. (Shiga gives a long account of this one
day in "One Page," written in 1909.)

At first he is very well pleased with his new life. Unfortunately
this euphoric state does not long continue. Within half a month he
is worn out again. His head is heavy, his shoulders are cramped, his
spirit is completely out of sorts. When he tries to sleep, he is visited
by frightening nightmares. Not only does the work not progress, but
he is even dissatisfied with what he has already done. He is restless
and does not know what to do with himself. He lies on the floor of
his room, thinking of Tokyo, or he wanders about the town with no
particular end in mind. Needless to say, the pleasurable state of excitement, which is the necessary condition for his writing, has
vanished completely. He passes day after day in even less
semblance of order than in Tokyo, and his condition grows worse
and worse.

Hoping to find some measure of relief, he takes a boat trip to the
island of Shikoku and about the islands of the Inland Sea. He has
several brief moments of pleasure, but he returns to Onomichi in as
bad a state as before.

To this point the story has been pure autobiography. Now the
fantasy begins. After his return he is at the point of despair. One
night he goes to the seashore away from the town and tries to give
out a mighty scream of anguish. But he has not even the strength
for this. He feels so sad that he is tempted to break down and cry
like a little child. "But I won't commit suicide," he thinks to
himself. He does not consider returning to Tokyo, for life there, he
realizes, would be no better.

Then one night he goes to a theater and sees there a beautiful girl
of about six, accompanied by her mother and grandmother. He is
completely captivated and cannot take his eyes off her during the
entire performance. He returns the following evening, hoping to
catch sight of her again. This evening she is with her father, and he
envies him. If he himself were a father, he could be satisfied with
nothing less than a daughter like this.

After this his spirits improve. He feels like a man who has just
fallen in love. He must have this girl for his own, so he decides to
kidnap her. He will be able to do more for her than her parents can.
His mind is now filled with these imaginings.

But when he returns to the theater the following evening, the girl is not in attendance; nor is she the following night or the one after that. He walks about the streets in search of her, but she is nowhere to be found. Troubled as he is by her sudden disappearance, he is even more troubled at the realization that he has no longer a very strong desire to go ahead with the kidnapping. Why, he wonders, should a desire once so strong wither away like this in so short a time? This too, he decides, is symptomatic of his disease.

He goes to have his aching shoulders massaged, and he decides to kidnap the masseur's daughter, though she is not beautiful like the other. A few days later he lures the girl with candy to his home. Even as he leads her to his door, he is repelled by her strong odor, "the odor of country children." He gets her into the house and gives her toys to play with. When she begins to cry for her mother, he tells her that her mother will come for her the following morning. He finally gets her to bed. He looks down at her as she sleeps, repelled by her foul-smelling hair and her light snoring. He himself goes to bed and dreams that he is being chased by the girl's father.

When he awakens, it is already one in the afternoon. The girl is still sleeping and wakes up a couple of hours later. He no longer finds anything attractive in her and realizes that he never loved her. But he will go through with his plan: take her to Tokyo and make her happy.

Soon the girl is crying. Afraid that people will hear her, he threatens her. She looks at him with hatred, and nothing he does can get her to change her expression. Looking at her hate-filled face, he realizes that his action was a piece of unforgivable egoism. He feels pity for both her and himself. "I began to cry. Suddenly she too was crying."

The following morning the girl's mother, accompanied by two policemen, comes for the girl. The hero thinks at first to resist but finds he has not the will to use the kitchen knife in his hand. Finally he is led away by the policemen.

Of this story, Shiga writes:

"The Kidnapping" is the product of my experience at Onomichi. Half of it is fact; the kidnapping and its aftermath are imagination. But it is a fact that I did have those imaginings. Since I was living by myself without a single friend, such imaginings played an important part in my daily life.

Even though they never came close to actualization, these imaginings were often present. If I were writing this story today, I would probably present it as mere imagination, but at that time I chose to write of it as if it had become fact. (X, 195—96)

This story, unsuccessful as it is, does give us a deep insight into Shiga's attitude toward life at the time of its writing. He wanted above everything to have a strong sense of self with which to confront the world, but this sense was already considerably weakened and had to be artificially stimulated. Thus, when the hero loses his strong desire of kidnapping the first girl, he tries to work himself up once again to his previous pitch, and it is this that motivates him to kidnap the masseur's daughter, in whom he really has no interest. It is this too that explains the strange fact that when he gets the girl into the house, the first thing he does is make the following entry in his journal (certainly a very strange action under the circumstances):

I finally went through with it. I finally did the terrible thing. I'm happy with myself for having been able to go through with it. There's no going back now. I have to go all the way. I don't know what the next move is, but at least I've done it. I've done what I had been unable to do however hard I tried. I have too low an opinion of myself. Now I have overcome that opinion. . . . If one only looks at what I have done, it seems to be but a bad whim. Bad whim or not, the future will decide. I must not try to defend myself before others. Even if I tried to do so, I probably could not. (II, 145)

But the hero has not really succeeded in conquering his low opinion of himself, as can be seen from the rest of the story. He admits to himself finally that what he did was a piece of unforgivable egoism. As a story, "The Kidnapping" is very confused and unsatisfactory, but it does portray quite vividly the condition in which Shiga found himself after his experience at Kinosaki.

VI   "Reconciliation" (1917)

In the summer of 1917 Shiga was finally reconciled with his father. "Reconciliation" was written immediately after the event.

The story begins with an account of Shiga's worsening relations with his father from a short time after his marrying without his father's consent. The father, desiring to be reconciled with his son, comes to visit him in Kyoto. Junkichi, the young man in this story, not wishing to meet his father, arranges to be away from home when he arrives, leaving it up to his already distraught wife to take care of him. The father is understandably angry, and returns to Tokyo feeling more bitter toward his son than before.

Because of Sadako's severe nervous condition, the young couple move to Abiko. One day they go to Tokyo to visit his grandmother. They intend to spend the night at the family home in Azabu, but late at night Junkichi is called to his father's room and asked to apologize for his rudeness to him in Kyoto. This Junkichi cannot do, though he feels quite differently toward his father now than he did then; and the father refuses to let the couple remain in his house overnight. They are forced to go to a hotel, where Sadako undergoes the humiliation of being regarded by the hotel staff as a woman of the night.

Some time later Sadako gives birth to their first child and goes to the home in Azabu to convalesce. The father is proud of his first grandchild and insists on paying all the medical expenses. Junkichi reluctantly accepts, but leaves it up to his wife to express their thanks. Junkichi is upset that the other members of the family look upon the child as a means of bringing father and son together. They take the child back to Abiko, but when the grandmother writes that Junkichi's father wishes to see the baby again, they make another trip to Tokyo with her. Upon their return to Abiko, the child falls ill and, despite all their efforts to save her, finally dies. Junkichi's grief at his daughter's death is further deepened by the realization that her death was indirectly caused by everyone's earnest desire to use the child as an instrument of reconciliation. The father sends word that the child should be buried in Abiko and not in the family plot in Tokyo. He refuses to have the coffin in his home and even prevents Junkichi's grandmother and little sisters from attending the funeral.

Life at Abiko after the child's death is extremely lonely and sad, and Sadako's condition grows worse. Once on a trip to Tokyo Sadako, but not Junkichi, stays at the family home. On this occasion the father becomes very angry with her, and Junkichi, hearing his wife's account of the incident, becomes still more resentful of his father.

The young couple's sadness turns to joy when they discover that

Sadako is pregnant again. In the meantime Junkichi's good friend
M (Mushakoji) has moved to Abiko, and his warm friendship and
constant encouragement have a healing influence on Junkichi. Hal-
cyon days follow and Junkichi comes to enjoy an ever-growing feeling of harmony and inner peace. He is even able to write again.
After the birth of the child, the only thing remaining to cloud his
spirit is the relationship with his father. His present sense of harmony and peace arouses a great desire for reconciliation.

Word reaches him that his grandmother is ill. He manages to visit
her a couple of times when his father is not home, but on one such
visit his father unexpectedly returns. Father and son do not even
speak to each other. On another visit, Junkichi's mother warns him
that worry over his relationship with his father is very bad for his
grandmother in her present condition, and urges him to write his
father a letter of reconciliation. Junkichi tries to do so but cannot;
he realizes that only a face-to-face meeting will do.

On his next trip to Tokyo Junkichi makes an arrangement to talk
to his father. He does not plan in advance what he will say, but
prefers to leave it to the natural inspiration of the moment. His
mother finds a chance to speak to Junkichi alone and begs him with
tears in her eyes to be gentle with his father. Junkichi replies that he
does not repent of anything he has done and that he cannot grovel
to his father. He will not apologize, for even if he did so, his heart
would not be in it and his father would be quick to realize this. "But
I'll go ahead and meet him," he tells her. "This is mostly a matter
of feeling. It's impossible to plan the interview in advance. Perhaps
when I come face to face with him my feelings may take a more
conciliatory turn than I now expect" (VI, 132).

The confrontation is described in the following passage:

> I rose and walked toward Father's room. I felt uneasy and of uncertain
> resolve. I didn't think it good to enter in this state of mind, so I walked up
> and down the corridor until I could compose myself. I gave no thought to
> how I would begin the conversation. It took about two minutes to calm my
> ruffled spirits. Then I approached the door of Father's study. . . . He was
> sitting at his desk facing me as I entered. His face was serene.
>
> "Take that chair." Father pointed to a chair by the window and in-
> dicated that I should set it in front of him. I did as he instructed and sat
> down facing him. I did not speak.

"Suppose you begin," he said. "Is Masa [Junkichi's uncle] in the other room?" His tone of voice made a good impression on me.

"Yes, he is," I replied. Father rose and rang the bell. Then he returned to his chair.

"Go on," he urged, since I still had not begun to speak. The maid entered and he had her call my uncle into the study.

"I don't think there's any sense in our going on like this."

"Yes?"

"Until now it couldn't be helped. I realize how hard this has been on you. I think I have been in the wrong in some things."

Father nodded. I was so excited that I sounded as if I were angry. This was quite a different tone from what my mother had urged me to take. ("Speak to him calmly and quietly," she had counseled.) But it was the tone most natural to me at that moment; and now in retrospect it seems to me to have been the tone best suited for speaking of our relationship. My uncle entered and took a chair behind me.

"Fine, but does what you say apply only as long as your grandmother is alive, or do you speak of something more lasting?" asked my father.

"Until I entered this room, I was not thinking of anything lasting. I wanted your permission for free access to this house as long as my grandmother was alive. But if it is possible to hope for more, that would be ideal." As I spoke, I fought back the tears.

"Is that so?" My father's lips were tightly clamped and tears were in his eyes. "I'm gradually getting old. It's been very painful to continue on such bad terms with you. It's a fact that I have even hated you at times. When you first spoke of leaving home and wouldn't listen to contrary advice, I was stunned. I had no choice but to agree, and yet I never once thought of kicking you out. And everything that has happened since. . ."

Father began to cry. I did too. Neither of us could say anything more. My uncle behind me began to say something, but before he could get out more than a few words he too was crying.

After a time Father rose and rang the bell. When the maid entered, he told her to call his wife. My mother came into the room and sat in a low chair at my father's side.

"Junkichi has just told me that he is also unhappy about the way things have developed and that he wants that we should return to our old intimacy as father and son. That's right, isn't it?" he asked, looking at me.

I nodded. Seeing this, my mother rose quickly and took firm hold of my hand. "Thank you, Junkichi, thank you," she said in tears, bowing to me again and again. As I bowed in return I couldn't help brushing my mouth against her hair when she raised her head. Then Mother went to my uncle's side and expressed her heartfelt thanks to him also.

"Go and tell Grandmother," Father told Mother. Mother quickly left the room, still crying. My four little sisters, including six-year-old Fukuko, entered. They stood together in a clump and bowed too. (VI, 132—35)

The last three sections of the story (this long story is divided into sixteen sections) depict the aftermath of reconciliation, the idyllic calm after the great storm.

Though "Reconciliation" may be considered a sequel to the earlier "Otsu Junkichi," the two stories represent the two opposite poles of the writer's sensibility. "Otsu Junkichi" was written when Shiga was most determined to make something of himself and to meet all obstacles head on, while "Reconciliation," as even the title suggests, shows him settling into an ever-deepening mood of harmony and peace, an ever-growing sense of union and reconciliation with both nature and man. It is this new mood, which began with the experience at Kinosaki after his encounter with death and became more pronounced in the course of his peaceful days at Abiko, that made reconciliation with his father seem imperative and moved him in this direction. And when reconciliation has finally been achieved, the harmony and peace become even more pronounced. After all the excitement, Junkichi feels extremely fatigued.

. . . but it was not an unpleasant fatigue. It was a fatigue accompanied by the kind of silence in which immediate objects recede into the distance, a fatigue that puts one in mind of a tiny pool, deep in the mountains, enveloped in mist. It was like the fatigue of a traveler who after a very long and unpleasant journey has finally reached home. (VI, 138)

This new sense of peace and harmony is particularly visible in one of the final scenes in which Junkichi goes to the station to see his father and sisters off after their visit to Abiko.

My father looked somewhat tired. The train pulled into the station. Everyone got on board. Father took a seat at the window opposite to the platform, where I remained standing, and my little sisters crowded into a seat at a window on the platform side and stood there, four faces in a row. When the whistle blew, they all said, "Good-bye." I bowed and tipped my cap, looking into the eyes of my father which were fixed on me. He muttered something and nodded, but I looked for something more from him. I kept staring into his eyes, very near to tears. Then suddenly a certain expression came over his face. It was this I had been looking for. I had been waiting for this without realizing it. With the excitement and pleasure of this meeting of our hearts, I was all the more dangerously close to tears. The train began to move. My sisters kept on waving until the train had left the platform and curved to the right out of sight. I stood for a long time alone, umbrella raised, on the deserted platform. Then coming to myself, I left the station and hurried home. I did not know why I was hurrying. I resolved that I would never again break this accord with my father. I now felt a deep affection for him, an affection in which all the many resentments of the past melted away. (VI, 140—41)

The story, despite its length, is essentially lyrical. Its exclusive aim is to present the writer's feeling. Shiga indicates as much in the following comment upon this work:

It was not my purpose to take as my theme the problem of morality in father-son relationships. Rather, this story was born out of a more direct emotion—the feeling of joy at a reconciliation reached at long last after so many years of discord. Therefore, I did not first pick out a theme and then start writing. I was impelled to write what I did by something much more direct. And it is here that the story has its power; it is for this reason that the reader is drawn into it. (X, 141—42)

From the story's lyrical conception spring both its excellence and its defects.

Most of the early readers of the story found it extremely moving. The Japanese philosopher Watsuji Tetsuro stated that he could "have no confidence in the literary taste of a person who was not deeply moved by the story, even to tears. Such a person cannot be said to have a heart."[4] In the same vein, the literary critic Kobayashi Hideo was certain that "readers of 'Reconciliation' will find that their eyes mist over with tears. That is because the writer's strong hold upon nature taps the source of our tears." The writer Eguchi Kiyoshi went so far as to state that "if there is anyone that calls this story sentimental, that person is very much to be pitied, inasmuch as he has absolutely no understanding for the beautiful sincerity which man is capable of possessing."

"Beautiful sincerity"—that is the key phrase in understanding the enthusiastic reception accorded this story. We have seen that "sincerity" was the great aim of both the Naturalist and the Shirakaba writers—the uncamouflaged presentation of the writer's "heart." But Shiga's "sincerity" in this story goes one step beyond that of most of the other writers, inasmuch as "Reconciliation" is a "sincere" account of a hero who lives with the greatest of "sincerity."

To say that the hero lives "sincerely" means, in this use of the word, that he is ruled in his actions by an ethics of feeling. In whatever he does, Junkichi refuses to go beyond his "felt realizations" *(jikkan)*. Even his desire for reconciliation he must entrust to the processes of nature. He cannot plan beforehand a course of reconciliation, since he may very well not have the right feeling for it when it comes time to act. Feelings cannot be anticipated. Emotions cannot be brought under the control of thought. He can see no other way but to wait until the emotions naturally take the desired route. What is forced and unnatural cannot be good, can only lead to further discord, even igniting the explosive element in a person. To try to anticipate feeling is to interfere with the natural process, and to disturb this is to disturb the very foundation of life, and thereby lose genuineness. To lose genuineness in life, further, is to lose genuineness also in one's writing, since only the words that issue from the genuine and true life can themselves be genuine.

It is for this reason that Junkichi refuses to meet his father in Kyoto, as he himself clearly states: "I could not possibly speak to my father as if nothing had happened, concealing the dissatisfaction I felt toward him at the time. I was sure that nothing would come out of deceiving myself and others. What would follow would be even worse than our present discord" (VI, 79).

It is for this reason too that Junkichi cannot find an ending for the story he has written about a father and son in similar conflict. He imagines their reconciliation at the dying grandmother's bedside, but he cannot trust his vision. He must first experience the reality himself before he can write about it. In this one stroke we are accorded a penetrating insight into Shiga's conception of literature and the degree to which it rejects all elements of fiction. The literary aim must always be "sincerity," and a writer can write "sincerely" only of what he himself has experienced.

Whatever one may think of Shiga's ideals of sincerity and genuineness as the most essential elements of literary composition, it cannot be denied that these are in great part responsible for the immediacy and vitality of a number of passages in the story. Most impressive is the account of the sickness and death of the first child and of the birth of the second. Perhaps no writer in any literature has better captured the purely natural aspects of the mystery of birth and death — dissociated, that is, from all philosophic reflection. Life and death are viewed as two moments of the same natural cycle, one inexorably bringing on the other.

In such passages the "felt realizations" *(jikkan)* of personal experience and the many excellences of Shiga's style—keen observation, accurate and lean description, rejection of the sentimental, and firm control—come together to constitute several of the finest pages of Shiga's writing, and indeed of Japanese literature.

It is when the story is considered as a whole that its defects become overwhelmingly apparent. In the first place, lyrically conceived as it was, it has too little regard for plot. The causes of the discord between father and son, for example, are never adequately explained. The writer seems to presume that the reader will know enough about his life to supply the details. Thus the emotional reactions of the hero and the other characters seem disproportionate to the cause, and therefore sentimental, inadequately motivated. Second, here as in Shiga's other autobiographical stories there is too close an identification between writer and hero, allowing little perspective for objective judgment.

A still more serious defect is that far too many details are given. Masamune Hakucho, one of the first Japanese writers to disagree with the general critical appraisal, wrote in 1928 that he had very little admiration for "Reconciliation," though it was undeniably well written and its descriptive prose well beyond the range of the average writer. What he objected to particularly was that the hero made so much of trifles. "I was annoyed by the hero's fussing over every trifling detail. He must touch upon every least thing that concerns him; he must pass judgment upon every word, every movement, every action. It is oppressive and unpleasant." Masamune also objects to the sentimentality of the scene of reconciliation.

The last scene in which everyone is weeping seems to have a lachrymose effect upon many readers. But I consider this scene no different from what one expects to find in a popular novel. One wonders why the writer of the

"The Old Man" could not have reported this episode in a similarly objective style. Perhaps because he is writing about himself and is too close to the event, he becomes overly self-indulgent. My own reaction was to feel annoyance at being asked to cry over complications of so trivial a nature.[5]

Masamune calls this and "Confused Head" the poorest of Shiga's works, though he admits having liked the scenes of the death and birth of the infants.

Edward Seidensticker goes one step further and explains why the details of the story give such a strong impression of being unnecessary trifles—because they have nothing to do with either character or plot development. Shiga makes use of them only because they actually occurred, not because he thinks it imperative that the reader know about them. The author imposes himself upon us and bids us consider important everything that has actually happened to him.[6] Such is the excess to which "sincerity" as a principle of literary composition must inevitably lead.

In final summation, it may be said—notwithstanding Masamune's harsher criticism—that "Reconciliation" is far superior to "Otsu Junkichi" and every other story we have taken up so far. Its defects are many, but individual passages are representative of modern Japanese prose at its very best. In these passages style conquers a defective philosophy of composition and the result is fine literature.

VII   "A Certain Man and the Death of His Sister" (1920)

Of the three stories "Otsu Junkichi," "Reconciliation," and "A Certain Man and the Death of His Sister," Shiga writes:

In their subject matter these are three branches of one and the same tree. While "Otsu Junkichi" and "Reconciliation" are almost purely autobiographical, "A Certain Man . . ." is a mixture of fact and fiction. . . . It was written after "Reconciliation," but as far as content goes, it should be placed before the latter. I wrote of the conflict between father and son as seen through the eyes of a younger brother. This and its other fictitious elements, such as the elder sister, place it at some distance from my actual experience, but I tried to depict as accurately as possible the psychology of my father and myself in our disagreement. I had the younger brother take a critical but sympathetic view of us. Though father and son both wish to be reconciled with each other, they finally are not.

"Reconciliation" is like a freshly caught fish; "A Certain Man . . ." is the same fish dried. It is a rather gloomy tale, not at all pleasant. I have very little liking for it, but I recall that I worked very hard on it. Even though I don't like it, I realize that it is a necessary part of my writing.[7]

Japanese critics generally take Shiga at his word. They treat "A Certain Man . . ." as a dried fish and largely ignore it. But the Western reader may very well find this story more to his taste than Shiga's other autobiographical pieces.

The three great defects noted in "Otsu Junkichi" and the other stories—the too close identification of author and hero, making for an oppressive subjectivity; poor organization of material; one-dimensional characters—are not so much in evidence here. In the first place, Shiga gains objectivity by using a third-person narrator that is sufficiently distant from the action to see it in perspective. This allows for a dramatic tension within and among characters: the son, the father, and even the grandmother are far more complex in this story than in the others in which they appear; and even the minor characters come to life. Second, Shiga has carefully organized his plot and even given it a frame, the scene of the sister's death with which the story begins and ends. He also makes use of contrast and symbol to tie the various parts of the story together.

The narrator of the story, Yoshizo, a man of thirty-two, recounts the history of his older brother's relationship with their father. He frames his story with an account of his last meeting with his brother at the deathbed of their sister in a remote country village. Yoshiyuki had run away from home nine years earlier and had not been seen or heard from since. After the sister's death he disappeared again, but Yoshizo is certain that he will appear at least one more time, when his grandmother will be on her deathbed.

As far back as Yoshizo can remember, his father and Yoshiyuki had never gotten on well. His explanation of the conflict is as follows:

Father and Brother were not bad people. On the contrary, they were extraordinarily honest. But at the same time stubborn. . . . When I reflect upon their characters, I realize how formidable a thing is blood heritage. I see that they had many traits in common. They differed only in the age to which they belonged and the circumstances of their lives. Both had a strong sense of self and plunged headlong without restraint in whatever direction they happened to be going. My father almost never had any doubt about the rightness of his course. With little or no hesitation he would go straight ahead and do what he wanted. But when Brother tried to do the same thing, he would soon encounter difficulties. The basic difference between the two was that my father, in the family circle at least, could always push his way through as he desired, while my brother generally could not. (Father would see to this.) . . . Still, however much anguish this may have caused him, my brother could never bring himself to substitute any other way for the one he had himself chosen. That was his nature. The harder it was to get his own way, the more intent he was upon getting it. (VI, 156)

Yoshizo gives many examples of their quarrels. Yoshiyuki tells his friends he will visit Kyoto with them; his father refuses to give him money since he had not taken the trouble to get his permission before committing himself. Yoshiyuki sells some books to a secondhand book store and goes anyway. Father is so angry that he hits Mother (Yoshiyuki's stepmother) with the brazier tongs for presuming to defend him. Again, Yoshiyuki asks financial help from his father to publish a collection of his short stories. This leads to an argument and the father proposes that Yoshiyuki live away from home for a time. He moves immediately, but returns home some weeks later. After a few months he decides to spend a year or so in Shodoshima (Onomichi in the other stories and in real life). On the day of his departure he lets his father leave the house for work without saying good-bye to him, though both are longing in their hearts for this final farewell. Then Yoshiyuki hurries to his grandmother's room and bursts into tears.

Yoshiyuki is determined to be a professional writer. His father, a successful businessman, has nothing but contempt for writers. This difference of attitude toward writing as a profession is the cause of many quarrels. Father invites Yoshiyuki to go with him to look at a farm he has just bought. He buys himself a first-class rail ticket and his son a second-class. Yoshiyuki on a trip with friends falls from a tree and is gravely injured. All the members of the family but Father go to see him at the hospital. Father really would have liked to go but couldn't bring himself to do so. It would have been too much like giving in, too much like hypocrisy.

In a letter to his sister, Yoshiyuki writes:

Father does nothing but grumble about me. He used to get angry because, according to him, I was too fond of extravagance. Then when I began to be more careful in my use of money, he would get angry at me because I was too lazy. I took to spending more time on my studies, but he still wasn't satisfied. He got angry now because I was always having my friends over and staying up late with them in "useless chatter." At this rate there is no end to the things he will find fault with. (VI, 208)

Yoshizo relates that the first great confrontation between father and son took place over the Ashio Copper Mine pollution incident. The second great battle occurred when Yoshiyuki set his mind upon marrying a family maid. Another major cause of the deteriorating relationship between father and son was the father's determination to choose a bride for his son. His standards were purely materialistic: the girl must be of a good and wealthy family. Girl after girl was rejected as not meeting this norm.

In spite of everything Yoshiyuki had a secret hunger for his father's love. Yoshizo reveals the complex nature of his brother's relationship with his father, his dead mother, and his grandmother.

If my brother's real mother were still alive, I wonder what kind of relationship he would have with her and with Father. Even a mother could never love him with such a strong, blind love as Grandmother does. My brother has himself said as much: "If Mother had lived, I doubt if she could have loved me with one-third of the love my grandmother has for me." Be this as it may, there was in him a hunger for a love that a grandmother could not completely satisfy. And this he tried to find in the imagined phantom of his lost mother. . . . Though almost sated by his grandmother's love, he looked for still more love. I think that he even sought for this love in Father, though he did not seem to be conscious of the fact.

At any rate, this was a source of anguish to him. Father was no more capable of giving him that kind of love than his dead mother. Still they were, after all, father and son. Buds have been known to sprout from a tree that has been abandoned as dead. It was not impossible that the love of father for son, which seemed to be dead, might in the warm sunlight of spring sprout new buds. How expectantly must Brother, who felt these buds alive in the deepest part of himself, have awaited that spring day when he would discover them also in the other. He even said as much to me. But finally that day never came. Father died first.

When he was younger, Brother would come angrily to Father and pick a quarrel with him over something or other. I'm sure that this was nothing but a strange manifestation of the frustration he felt at not being able to receive the affection from him he so greatly desired. My brother in those days cried a lot. With tears in his eyes he would say rude things to Father. As these attacks increased, Father gradually came to avoid all contact with him. When Brother came to speak with him about something, he would say, "If we discuss this further, we'll only end up in a fight. So I have nothing to say." And he made an ugly face, showing how distasteful he found the conversation. But even then, Brother pursued the topic with strange tenacity. "Go away, go away," Father would say, as if he were shooing away a dog. Brother still wouldn't leave. Then Father would walk out into the garden, but Brother would follow him even there. Finally Father would leave the house, and Brother would run up to his room and cry. (VI, 159–60)

How much better a story "Reconciliation" would have been if the complexity of the relationship between father and son described so objectively in the above passage had been introduced there. Then the reconciliation between father and son would have been more moving.

Later, Yoshizo continues, his brother was able to assume an attitude of indifference. If he had had this attitude earlier, or else if he had not had such a deep longing for his father's love, their relations would never have reached the breaking point as they did.

Yoshizo points to another factor complicating the relations of father and son. Yoshiyuki had been raised by his grandparents. Moreover, his grandfather was for long the gracious but firm patriarch ruling over the family. Both of these circumstances tended to put father and son on much the same level, as if they were brothers separated by a gap of years who did not get on well with each other.

Perhaps for this reason Father could never speak to my brother with paternal ease and assurance. He had to oppose him, to pick a quarrel with him. . . . He would never give in to him on any count. To give in, he must have felt, was to suffer defeat. (VI, 211)

When Yoshiyuki does finally leave home, however, it is not in rage at his father. He has passed through that stage to a better understanding of himself. He has come to realize that if he is to find his own way and lead the kind of life that is suited to him—in other words, if he is to be faithful to himself—he must get out. He writes to his sister:

I am the one that is at fault. Only me. It is right that someone like me should not be loved by Father. . . . I've got to make a complete break. . . . But please don't worry about me. I am leaving home because I have long wanted to live in a way that will allow me to be myself. . . . At present only my relations with Father occupy the center of my vision. I know very well that this is not the whole of life. (VI, 214–15)

Almost all the drama in Shiga's work, as we have already seen, derives, directly or indirectly, from his long-continuing struggle with his father. "A Certain Man . . ." presents this relationship more dramatically, more objectively, and with greater complexity (and conversely, with less sentimentality) than it is presented in his other works. Because of the element of fiction, which Shiga so disliked, this story is not just a string of personal recollections, moving, perhaps, but hardly more than a memoir; it takes on a greater universality and becomes something closer to everyone's experience of the complexity of family relationships and the tragedy that can result therefrom. In this regard, notice the rightness of Shiga's dramatic sense in having the father die before reconciliation could be achieved.

A good example of the heightening effect of the fictitious element in the story is the account of the sister's death, which is used to frame the narrative. She had been a beautiful girl of twenty when she married her husband, a subordinate of her father's at the company at which they were employed, and greatly trusted by him. When the father learns that the husband has embezzled a considerable sum of money from the firm, he refuses ever to see him or his daughter again (unless she separates from him, which, being a faithful wife and the mother of two children, she will not do). The father has never relented from his stern decision. He has even prevented the other members of the family from seeing her. Even when word of her critical condition reaches the family, he will not let them go to see her. (She is living in a little farming village in a remote part of Japan.) Finally, he does permit the younger brother to make the journey.

The final scene of the novel, depicting the death of the sister, is an example of Shiga at his best. (Shiga is always good at describing

scenes of birth and death.) With his sharp eye for detail, he makes
the reader feel the tragedy of the sister's life and, by implication, of
the father's character, since it is because of his unreasonable decree
that she is here, removed even from medical help.

There is the poignancy, first of all, of the brothers meeting accidentally on the road to the village. Though Yoshizo has so much
he wants to say to his brother, they walk together in silence.

After all, he was my brother. I was deeply moved. And he seemed to be too.
This made it all the more difficult for us to speak. For my grandmother and
my parents also there were so many things to say and ask. But it seemed
bad manners and somehow unnatural to do so now. So I didn't touch upon
these topics. All I could say was, "Have you been well?" and "Have you
come from a long distance?" and the like. (VI, 223)

They reach the farmhouse, one of only six in the tiny village.
They are greeted by their sister's husband, his mother, and the two
children, and are ushered into the sickroom. Shiga gives a very good
description of the deep gloom of the scene.

My brother sat beside the bed, looking silently at her face. She seemed to
be unconscious. When I saw her sunken eyes and her dry skin, the color of
dirt, I could hardly bear it. I was filled with a feeling that was something
more than fear at the thought that a person's life had to end in this way. If
one must die, one way of dying is as good as another, I suppose. But this
scene was already too much like the world of the dead: just the one small
lamp suspended from the ceiling of the strangely large room, which was
discolored by smoke; nothing of a bright color to be seen; no color or
human warmth even in the attitude of the husband and the mother-in-law.
If this same deathbed had been in a room, say, at the Akasaka Red Cross
Hospital, I probably would not have found death half so fearful. There
would have been flowers, white walls, white sheets, and people bidding a
tearful farewell to the dying; and these would all have alleviated the fear.
But there were none of these things here. I felt the fear of death just as if
death were a falling into an endless darkness, the kind of feeling one
sometimes has as one is falling asleep. The fact that there would be a
morrow, when birds would be singing, insects flying, wind blowing, sun
shining, flowers blooming, and dogs running about, never even occurred to
me. I felt that if death were eternal darkness, then life was like the dusk of a
cold day on a high mountain plateau. At least, that is what it had been for
my sister. (VI, 225)

Yoshizo confesses that he would have found the scene even more frightening had his brother not been there with him. He felt his brother to be his one support, especially his eyes, "eyes which put up no resistance to death, but at the same time would never be vanquished by it." In this one phrase is expressed the attitude toward death that is to be found in all of Shiga's scenes of death.

The next day is clear and windless, with an autumn sun streaming into the sickroom, dispelling the gloom of the previous evening. After breakfast Yoshizo takes his thirteen-year-old nephew, Masao, into the woods and tries to learn what plans he has made for his life. But Masao has only one desire, to own a rifle. When they return to the house, a local lantern maker is giving the dying sister a *moxa* treatment. He explains that since "all illness is caused by the accumulation of evil humors in the body," it is necessary to cauterize in order to let these humors out. This is the only "doctor" whose services have been available to her.

The sister regains consciousness. She looks about the room, but does not recognize her brothers. She tries to speak, and they finally make out that she is asking them to change the bedding so that she will not die on the good quilts reserved for guests and dirty them. Shortly afterward she dies.

Shiga is very good at describing the activities that follow death: all the relatives except the husband crying, the villagers gathering, the wives preparing a large meal, the young men carrying in the coffin from the barn, the daughter sitting at her dead mother's side and periodically lifting the white cloth over her face to see if she is not still alive, all the men talking loudly and drinking sake.

The sister's body is very dirty, and the brothers wash at least the face. There is one spot below the ear that will not come clean, however hard Yoshiyuki rubs. He has to be reminded that the spot is a birthmark, and he recalls how charming he had once found this mark. The transition from charming birthmark to grimy stain is an apt symbol for the extreme reversal in the sister's life and circumstances.

There is a wake that evening. The next morning when Yoshizo gets up he finds that his brother, without saying anything to anyone, has already departed, and he regrets that he has not had the chance to really talk with him. There the story ends.

This is one of the finest stories Shiga ever wrote. The reader cannnot but regret that Shiga was prevented from writing many more such stories by his peculiar philosophy of composition, his notion of "sincerity" as the principal element of all good writing.

VIII   *The Yamashina Stories (1925—26)*

We have already discussed the Yamashina affair in the opening chapter. The details of the affair are recounted by Shiga in a series of four stories, "Recollections of Yamashina," "Blind Passion," "A Trifling Incident," and "Late Autumn."

"Recollections of Yamashina" begins with the hero on his way home from a tryst with the waitress. He is thinking of the woman from whom he has just parted and is still relishing the pleasure of their meeting. But as he approaches his home, a cloud comes over his spirit as he thinks of the lie he must tell his wife. It makes him angry that he must thus assume the stance of a weakling.

> He loved his wife. Even after he had begun to love this other woman, his love for his wife had not changed. To love a woman other than his wife was something unusual for him. The very unusualness of it had acted as a strong attraction drawing him into the affair. He thought that it might afford a lively stimulus to his stagnating life. He realized that this was a pragmatic consideration, but he didn't think that his action could be considered evil. (III, 198)

He feigns a nonchalant air as he rings the bell, opens the gate, and enters his home, but his spirit is in gloom as he reflects upon his deception. His wife, who is always quick to greet him at the door, does not do so today. He finds her huddled in the bedding laid out in a corner of the room. She pushes her head out of the covers and turns her tear-stained eyes toward him. He realizes immediately that she knows everything.

There follows one of the most unusual confrontations that can be imagined between philandering husband and deceived wife:

> He became excited, then angry. Silently he returned his wife's stare. He could not speak until she did.
> "I thought something was odd, and when I telephoned I discovered that I was right. . . . And you promised there would never be such a thing. You really had me fooled." She got out from the covers and sat in the middle of

the room.

He felt like shouting at her, but he couldn't find the right words. He stared at her sternly. Her face wore a smile of disgust and was so red that he thought she must have a fever.

"You have a fever." He came close to her and put his hand to her forehead.

"That doesn't matter," she said, brushing his hand aside roughly. Her eyes, which always had a soft look, were now glaring fiercely into his. He wanted to avert her gaze, but instead he resolutely took the offensive.

"This is none of your concern. It has absolutely nothing to do with you."

"What? Who does it have more to do with than me? Why do you say it is none of my concern?"

"If you didn't know about it, it would be of no concern to you. Even with this, my feeling toward you hasn't changed the least bit." He knew that his words were egotistic, but he had indeed discovered, to his pleasure, that even after falling in love with this woman, his love for his wife had undergone no change.

"That's not true. That's not true at all. What was one until now has been divided into two . . ."

"Feelings are not like figures."

"You're wrong." She became hysterical and slapped his hand. He repeated that he had not the slightest feeling of infidelity to her.

"If you didn't have a feeling of infidelity, such a thing could never have taken place."

He was not lying. It was unpleasant to have to defend himself like this. (III, 199—200)

He regrets only that he has made her unhappy. His excuse lies in the fact that his feeling for her is "sincere." She answers that the greater the sincerity of his feeling for her, the greater the guilt of his infidelity.

Could there be anything more convincing than this passage in revealing the inadequacy of Shiga's ethics of feeling and exaggerated esteem of "sincerity"? This moment, writes Nakamura Mitsuo, finally puts an end to Shiga's long adolescence.[8] His frank narration of this incident with all it implies is perhaps a sign that he was already on his way to the maturity and humanity that characterized the later Shiga.

The story does not end at this point. In a second section the husband skillfully maneuvers the conversation so that it is the wife who has now to defend herself for her behavior — completely innocent

—on another occasion, a most ungentlemanly piece of strategy that
further lowers the stature of the hero in the eyes of the reader.
Finally he agrees, though reluctantly, to break with the waitress.

At the beginning of the second story, "Blind Passion," the husband has not yet broken with O-Kiyo, the teahouse waitress. He
even regrets that he has promised to do so. Though the woman, he
knows, feels no attachment to him, he is strongly drawn to her.
Even if he should resolve never to see her again, he does not think
he is strong enough to be able to keep his resolution. Still, it is
equally unpleasant to go on deceiving his wife. If only she would
generously give him permission to continue seeing the woman. He
had considered this a possibility at one time, but he realizes now
that that was but a delusion.

His wife was demanding that he settle the matter this very day,
and he was resigned to making at least the gesture of parting from
her. "All you have to do is pay her off," she tells him. He realizes
that his wife, filled as she is with a sense of having been betrayed
and deceived, is not her usual self and that what she says is undoubtedly correct; but such a show of contempt for another person
is so unlike her that he is shocked and angry. He assures himself
once again that his feeling for his wife has not changed, has perhaps
even improved.

The woman in question is a large, mannish woman of about
twenty or twenty-one, with nothing at all of the spiritual in her. He
does not understand how he could have fallen in love with her. It
had been so unexpected. He found in her the taste of fresh fruit that
his wife had long lost. He felt a certain amount of disgust with
himself inasmuch as his interest, he realized, was entirely on the
sensual plane, but stronger than the disgust was the feeling of attraction, and he had been able to concentrate on the latter and ignore the former.

His wife enters the room and continues to press him for an immediate settlement. She proposes to go with him. He urges her to
take care of herself since she has a slight fever. She replies, "I don't
care if I get sick. Besides, that's what you want, isn't it? That I get
sick and die?" He gets angry and his language becomes abusive.
She too rises to the attack.

"You don't think of anyone but yourself, do you? . . . You're very good at criticizing others. But taking a critical look at yourself is another matter. Why should that be? When the children tell lies and such, you scold them, perhaps too severely, but you don't seem to have any qualms about telling lies yourself."

"I tell the truth whenever I can. I hate to tell lies. If I thought you could stand the truth, I would never lie to you." . . .

". . . But you told me the whole truth last night, didn't you? You're not still hiding something, are you? That's fine. I want a firm promise from you for the future. That you will never do such a thing again. Please make me believe that you won't. I'll forget about all that has taken place. But make me believe it. Will you do that?"

"I don't know. Even this affair began so unexpectedly that I don't see how I can vouch for the future."

She became excited and shouted, "Then I can't go on living."

"What will you do, if you can't go on living?"

"Oh, I won't commit suicide, but I'm sure that I will die a natural death. I'm certain of it."

Since his wife had such strong feelings on the matter, he had no choice but to part with the other woman, at least for the time being, but the thought of it made him angry. (III, 208–209)

He goes to make the settlement. The woman cries when he tells her. He draws her "large, heavy body" into his lap and embraces her. Her mouth is salty from her tears and remembering that his wife's mouth the previous evening had also been salty from crying, he reflects how unlike him it is to have two such women on his hands.

He gives her the money and leaves. Though the matter is now settled, his feeling for the woman remains the same. She had asked him to come just once more and he had given her an ambiguous answer. He had no desire to part from her like this; he feels that he really must see her again.

That night his wife takes to her bed with a cold and she does not get better for many days. Worse than her illness is her nervous condition. She is always in a state of excitement, his infidelity always on her mind. She asks repeatedly for assurances that this affair is really over. He tells her what she wants to hear, but he realizes himself that his voice somehow lacks conviction. He wants to get away from her and thinks of business he has in Tokyo. But he no sooner reaches Tokyo than he receives a letter from her saying that the affair is always on her mind and asking him never, never to give her such an experience again. While he is still reading the letter, he receives a telegram from her begging him to come home and he does so immediately.

In the third story, "A Trifling Incident," the husband, still half infatuated with the waitress, goes once again to meet her, unknown, of course, to his wife. Fortunately or unfortunately, she is away with another man. On his way home, however, he catches a glimpse of the two and is even pleased to see her with the other.

Shiga, hard pressed to meet a deadline for a promised story, was indiscreet enough to submit "A Trifling Incident," and despite his precautions his wife came to lay eyes upon it, thus learning that the affair was not completely closed. Her reaction to this latest provocation is recounted in the story "Late Autumn." The husband assures her that this time he will make a complete break. He actually does so, and the story ends upon a note of reconciliation.

As can be seen from the above, there was nothing at all of the spiritual in the husband's infatuation with the waitress. He neither asks for her love, nor does he give her his. There is only lust and he is aware of this. In "Blind Passion" he even goes so far as to justify his action on the grounds that in the world of prostitution, prostitution is morality. But what this signifies is that in his relationship to O-Kiyo he too observes the morality of the world of prostitution. He is the exploiter, the dirty old man. Here again the inadequacy of Shiga's ethics of feeling is shown up for what it really is—the grossest of egoisms.

He himself comes to realize this. In "Late Autumn" the wife tells the husband, "You are completely self-centered," and he recognizes the truth of her words and is pained by it.

IX   "Kuniko" (1927)

Just as Shiga had fictionalized the material of his long-continuing conflict with his father in the story "A Certain Man and the Death of His Sister," so he now did the same with the material of the Yamashina affair. The result was the story "Kuniko." As fiction, the story is not among his best, but as autobiography, it affords a still deeper insight into the mind of Shiga Naoya at the most critical point of his literary career.

The hero of "Kuniko" is a middle-aged dramatist whose wife has just committed suicide, leaving behind her husband and three little children. Though he loved her deeply, he realizes that he is responsible for her death, and he is writing this story to put in order what he has experienced and to try to understand the nature and gravity of his guilt.

Kuniko had come from a very poor family and was a waitress at a summer resort when he first met her. He was still a bachelor at thirty-six and had had relations with a number of women. He had thought to prey also upon Kuniko, but instead he had fallen in love with her and married her. They had many happy and peaceful years together. Then one day he casually mentioned to her that several years earlier he had had relations with the maid while she was away. He was unprepared for her violent reaction. She had thought that he was different from the "beasts" she had met while working as a waitress. Now she is disillusioned and shocked. He tells her that he too was a "beast" before marriage and that he cannot even now say with certainty that he is not. In every man there is the beast.

"Beast" is probably too strong an expression, but for a man what comes first is his work, then his love for a woman. That is instinct with him. His way of loving may often give the impression of being animal-like. . . . Of course, I am not proud of my behavior. I feel as if I have done you a wrong, but as far as I alone am concerned, my conscience hardly troubles me. That is not to say that what I did was good, . . . only that my conscience has become habitually dulled. (IV, 53–54)

Kuniko tries to wrest a promise from him that he will never do that sort of thing again, but all he can tell her is that he will try to avoid all occasions of such conduct. She is not satisfied with this. His frankness has opened a crack in her "globe of happiness," especially since her happiness, like that of most women, has been built upon an illusion.

Another four years go by without event, except that the dramatist has reached a total impasse in his work. He cannot write and spends his days in idleness. A critic has written that he is troubled with too much family peace, that he is too snug in his cozy world;[9] and he himself agrees with the diagnosis. In his excess of peace he feels as if he has fallen into a mudswamp and cannot find a foothold to free himself. Everything bores him and he begins to look about for something unusual to divert him.

Just at this time a certain theatrical group decides to stage one of his plays. In the course of the negotiations and rehearsals, he becomes involved with one of the actresses in the play. He is able to keep his wife in ignorance of the fact for several months, but one day his picture with the actress appears on the society page of the newspaper and his secret is out. The scene that follows his wife's discovery is largely a repetition of the one in "Recollections of Yamashina." The hero of this story, however, is less attached to the other woman than the husband in the earlier stories. He breaks with her immediately.

Strangely enough, this affair has had the desired effect on his writing. The family crisis releases his pent-up talents and he is able to take up again the lengthy work he had begun long before but had never been able to finish (*Journey Through Dark Night* in real life). He plunges himself into his work and forgets all about his wife and children. He spends all his days in his study and sees his family only at mealtimes. When he is with them, he is always in bad temper so that his wife is afraid to speak to him and begins to tiptoe around the house for fear of disturbing him. He presses her harder and harder, and even tells her that he will go away for half a year to complete his work in quiet.

One night as he is at work in his study, he hears her moving back and forth in her room beneath him, though it is past two o'clock in the morning. Then there is silence. And then he hears someone creeping up the stairs. When the door to his room opens, he says, without looking, "I can't talk to you now." When he finally does turn toward her, he sees that her face is like a death mask, as if no longer of this world. She throws herself at his feet and clings to him. Then he realizes that she has taken poison. He tries to save her, but it is too late. She dies, writhing in great pain on the floor of his study.

This story is the product of Shiga's mature reflections upon the meaning that the Yamashina affair had for him as family man and writer. He shows in great detail the state of mind that propelled him toward the affair and the effect it had upon both his inner and outer life. The story is more philosophic and less immediate than the earlier stories and therefore of interest mainly as a guide for understanding the transformation Shiga underwent at this time.

Shiga tried to make the characters as different as possible from his wife and himself. The hero is a dramatist; the wife is from a poor and vulgar background and has been abused by men before her marriage. But the psychology of the two main characters is clearly that of Shiga and his wife at the time of the Yamashina affair.

The possibility that Shiga's wife might commit suicide over the Yamashina affair seems to have been real enough. She continued to brood over the affair for a long time thereafter. In "Kuniko" Shiga imagines the worst possible consequences that could have arisen from his indiscretion, in order to put himself into the proper frame of mind for repairing the damage that had been done to his family. By conjuring up these possible consequences, he was able to exorcise his fears and return to an equable state of mind.

The husband pretends to be repentant and is writing the story so that he can come to a realization of the precise nature of his guilt. But this realization he never really achieves. To the very end he remains bewildered. He has been faithful to himself and his code of life, and yet tragedy has issued from his action. The most he is finally able to accuse himself of is not having been sensitive enough to the condition of his wife's nerves. All that he is certain of at the end is that Kuniko has taken her own life and he is grieved by it. There is no hint of the nature of his repentance or of its source or to what it is directed.

In the following passage we see the hero (Shiga) struggling toward an understanding of the relationship between life and art:

When Shimazaki Toson was writing *The Broken Commandment* some twenty years ago, he stated that he was resolved to complete this work at any sacrifice. He was prepared to scrimp as much as possible on living expenses, to see his family go hungry and his daughters die off one by one. When I read this I became very angry. I wanted to ask if *The Broken Commandment* were really worth so much. To sacrifice several daughters for it is no small price to pay. There was more involved here, I thought, than just the writing of *The Broken Commandment*.

But I'm sure that others can say the same of me. "Whether a dramatist like you is able to bring to life in his work only one woman character or many is a question of little meaning to us. [One of the hero's motives for entering upon the affair with the actress was his awareness of the fact that the only woman he knows well enough to make live in his work is his wife.] What is more important is that you do not cause the least unhappiness to this one woman. Go on breeding your fish, repairing the paper panels of your home, and raising beautiful dahlias. Even if you never write another thing, other younger dramatists will emerge, one after the other. No one really cares what happens to you as a writer."

Were I an objective observer, that is probably what I would have to say. But returning now to my own point of view, I cannot easily agree with that sentiment. Dramatists of my stamp are not so numerous in any age. I hate the word *genius*, but if men of rare and special talents can be said to be geniuses, then I am certainly a genius. I still have a long way to go before I perfect my talents. If I end here, work that was destined to be given to the world will remain buried forever. I should not be living the life I am. (IV, 61−62)

These are his reflections before breaking away from the peace and boredom of his happy married life and entering upon the affair with the actress. In the light of Kuniko's death, however, he reflects: "But I might have been happier if I had continued to lead the life I was leading, if I had ended up an ordinary citizen, untalented and unfruitful. So it seems to me now that Kuniko is dead" (IV, 62).

That is, in a sense, what happened. "Kuniko," states Nakamura, is Shiga's last will and testament as a writer. He published nothing for the next five years and he wrote little that was significant thereafter.

CHAPTER 4

Journey Through Dark Night

SHIGA Naoya's most ambitious autobiographical work and his only long novel is *Journey Through Dark Night*. Though it lacks the perfection of his best short stories, it is generally considered to be his finest and most representative work. "Here," writes Agawa Hiroyuki, "is to be found everything Shiga possesses, everything that he aspired to in his life and work."[1] Some Japanese critics go so far as to call it the highest peak of modern Japanese literature. Western critics in general are far less enthusiastic, but also find much to praise in the work. The novel has gone through many editions and was the favorite of successive generations of Japanese youth, though it seems to have little popularity with the present generation.

Shiga put much of his lifeblood into this work. Under its earlier title, *Tokito Kensaku*, it was begun shortly after he had published his first short stories and sketches, in 1912, and it was not completed until 1937, twenty-five years later. The themes and moods of most of his best work are somewhere to be found in this long, sprawling novel. Moreover, he wrote nothing of any great literary significance after its completion. Thus *Journey Through Dark Night* is truly a compendium of Shiga Naoya, man and writer.

The novel consists of a prologue and four parts. In spite of the years it took to reach completion, it covers a period of only some five years, from approximately 1912 to 1917 (with the exception of the prologue, which consists of the hero's childhood recollections).

I *Prologue and Part I*

In the prologue the hero, Tokito Kensaku, reminisces about his childhood. As far back as he can remember his father was indifferent to him and even at times seemed to hate him. His mother, he realizes now, loved him, but she was always scolding. He admits

that he was self-willed and in need of reprimand, but all too often
he was singled out for rebuke when his brothers and sisters were as
guilty as he. He grew so accustomed to this kind of injustice that he
did not even question it, and he took for granted that it would continue throughout his life.

At the age of six his mother died and a grandfather he had never
met suddenly made his appearance and took him to live in his
house. This grandfather, a disreputable, vulgar old man always surrounded by equally disreputable and vulgar friends, Kensaku found
it impossible to love or even to respect. Kensaku did become deeply
attached, however, to his grandfather's mistress, a much younger
woman by the name of O-Ei.

At the beginning of Part I the grandfather is dead. Kensaku is living alone with O-Ei and trying to establish himself as a writer. He
has little contact with his father, but his older brother, Nobuyuki,
with whom he has a warm relationship, enters the picture often as
adviser and consoler. This first part portrays the young writer's
progressive descent into a life of idleness, irregularity, dissipation,
and finally debauchery.

Between the events of the prologue and those of Part I, Kensaku
had fallen in love with a childhood friend, the daughter of an aunt
by marriage, but when he had asked to marry her, his proposal had
been rudely rejected. Since he could think of no possible reason for
such an offhand rejection, he had been deeply hurt. More than disappointment in love, it was the sense of betrayal that he felt most
keenly. The incident has shaken his faith in men and has made it
difficult for him to place his trust in others.

In his quest for diversion Kensaku begins to frequent the
teahouses of Yoshiwara (in Tokyo) and engage in insipid conversation and childish games with the geisha there. One or two attract
him, and he fancies himself to be in love, but closer approach brings
disillusionment. His visits to the teahouses become more and more
frequent and he is away from home two or three days at a time,
moving from one teahouse to another. This, of course, requires
money, and he is soon pawning his books and other personal
possessions. But, far from diversion, all he experiences is boredom.
Finally, feeling a compulsion toward stronger stimulation, he sets
out "on a cold, cloudy morning . . . not on impulse, but with full
purpose and determination" for a brothel. He emerges two hours

later feeling "light and at ease."

Far from settling him, however, this further stage of degeneration makes him all the more discontent with his life. His carnal desires, thus unleashed, fix themselves upon O-Ei. He has her constantly on his mind; she becomes the center of his sexual fantasies. Still, he has the vague feeling that if he were to have relations with her, it would lead to destruction. She is, after all, twenty years his senior and has been his grandfather's mistress.

At the end of Part I Kensaku has resolved to break out of his circle of dissipation and go away somewhere where he can lead a simple life and do some writing. He decides upon Onomichi.

II   *Part II*

The quiet life and beautiful scenery of Onomichi are agreeable to Kensaku at first. With a peace of soul and a self-composure he has not experienced for a long time, he begins to write his *magnum opus,* an autobiographical work that is to encompass his entire life from childhood to the present. But soon the old malaise returns. The monotony of the life in this small town and the feeling of isolation and solitude begin to oppress him. All his days are the same and he misses his friends. His health, too, deteriorates; he has no appetite and is unable to sleep. He realizes that he is ailing in body and spirit. He has reached an impasse in his writing and cannot continue with the novel.

He seeks relief from this condition by making a trip around the islands of the Inland Sea. This serves but to deepen his depression. Only the thought of marrying O-Ei promises a measure of relief from his present condition. He returns to Onomichi and writes to his brother, Nobuyuki, asking him to convey his proposal of marriage to O-Ei. The prospect of marriage with her stirs up his passions again and he begins once more to seek out prostitutes. Nobuyuki's answer to his letter strikes him a double blow: it informs him that O-Ei has refused his proposal of marriage and that Kensaku is not the son of the man he has always taken to be his father but is the offspring of an illicit relationship between his mother and his "grandfather." Kensaku is stunned at the revelation. He is struck with horror as he contemplates this act that brought him into the world. But he experiences also a sense of relief in knowing the reason for the special treatment he has received from childhood and also for his cousin's refusal to marry him. While he feels even more repelled than before by his "grandfather," he detects in himself at the same time the buds of something resembling filial affection toward him.

As might be expected, Nobuyuki's revelation plunges Kensaku into still deeper darkness. Falling further and further into the dark, he has no resilience to wage opposition; he can but abandon himself to it. At this pitch of despair he determines that his writing will be his salvation. Because of this frightening inheritance, there are probably seeds of evil implanted in him too, but he will fight to keep them from germinating. He decides that he must reform his life and make greater efforts to control his carnal desires if he is to conquer these seeds of evil. But, knowing how weak he is, he has little confidence that he can keep his resolution.

He returns to Tokyo. Afraid of the fearful fate that may await him if he marries his real father's mistress, he gives up all thought of marrying O-Ei. In Tokyo Kensaku's motives for leading an orderly life grow dimmer with the passing of the days, and he is strongly tempted to return to the old life of dissipation. He is no longer moved by the ideal of working as an artist for the happiness of mankind and the progress of man. Finally, he feels there is but one place that will receive him. On the streetcar to the brothel he looks at the faces of the people in the car and realizes that he is the most miserable person there. In contrast to the others, there is no blood coursing through his veins and his eyes are those of a dead fish. The second part ends with Kensaku playing with the breasts of a prostitute and crying out, "A bumper crop! A bumper crop!" This was all that could fill the vacuum of his existence; this was all there was of value in the world.

III   *Part III*

At the beginning of Part III Kensaku has been in Kyoto for a month. The therapy of the old temples and their splendid art is effecting his convalescence from the sense of desolation he had experienced in Tokyo. On one of his walks about the city he catches sight of a young lady who seems to be nursing an elderly couple. He walks past her house again and again, and he decides that this is the girl he must marry. With her at his side his dark life will become bright again. Without having exchanged so much as a word with her, he arranges for an intermediary to present his marriage proposal. While awaiting the results of these negotiations, he travels to Nara and Ise and stops at the village in which his mother was born. He is sad to discover that no one there knows anything about her and her family, and he concludes that the line must begin all over again with him, that he is now the "ancestor."

O-Ei comes to say good-bye to him. She is going to Manchuria where she has decided to invest her savings in a teahouse owned by her cousin and to help with the management of the place.

Word finally comes that the girl, Naoko, will marry him, and they choose an early date for the wedding. It is only then that he has his first face-to-face encounter with her. The meeting could not have been more disastrous. She had spent the previous day on a train, traveling from her native village, and had been too tired and excited to get any rest the night before. Today she has a headache and an upset stomach. Naturally enough under the circumstances, Kensaku receives quite a different impression from that of before. He had idealized her beyond all proportion as the woman who best suited him. Now he finds fault even with her hairdo, which strikes him as too old-fashioned. Kensaku is never good at talking to people that he is meeting for the first time, and today he is more than usually tired and nervous and can think of nothing to say. They go to a theater performance. All through the performance his eyes are on her rather than on the play, and he marvels that this could be the same girl that he set his heart upon two months earlier. He can hardly wait for the evening to end and, when it finally does, he escapes with something of the feeling of a bird that has been let out of its cage.

He feels that this is a bad start for their marriage. But he is more worried about his own habits of debauchery, which he blames not only upon himself but also upon the seeds of evil he has inherited from his "grandfather." He decides that he has to pull himself together. He feels that if he does not start to lead a proper life now, he will not be able to avoid doing something that will eventually lead to his destruction. He renews the resolution that he has made and broken so often in the past.

Kensaku and Naoko are married a few days later in a simple ceremony attended only by a few relatives and friends. Despite their inauspicious first meeting, the two are happy together in their married life. They often go walking about Kyoto and visiting temples. Kensaku experiences a happiness and peace he has never known before—too much peace, perhaps, for he still finds it impossible to write. Naoko is soon pregnant and both await in great anticipation the birth of the child. The child finally arrives. Mother and child are doing well and Kensaku is happy, though he has difficulty realizing he is a father.

The eighth day after birth the baby takes ill and will not stop crying. The illness is diagnosed as erysipelas. Despite the best of care, the child develops cellulitis ten days later and an operation becomes necessary. The pair spend horrible days and still worse nights as the child lies suspended between life and death. In spite of its strong will to live, the baby finally dies, one month after birth. Its death is particularly hard on Naoko, who does not quickly recover from it.

Kensaku tries to return to his writing, but he feels something heavy weighing down on him and he cannot write.

IV   *Part IV*

For a long time after his child's death, Kensaku's days are filled with a strange loneliness and foreboding. He cannot dismiss the tragedy as mere accident, but discerns in it a mystifying element of purpose. He is distracted from his own suffering for a time when he goes to Seoul to bring back O-Ei, who has been deceived by her cousin and is stranded penniless in that city.

When he arrives back at Kyoto with O-Ei, he is surprised to find that Mizutani, an acquaintance whom he dislikes, is on the station platform with Naoko to welcome him back. He is further displeased to hear that Naoko's cousin, Kaname, has spent three nights in his house during his absence and has even had Mizutani over for an all-night card game. He senses intuitively that something is wrong; Naoko is stiff and ill at ease. When they arrive home, however, she is again her usual self. He scolds her for permitting her cousin and Mizutani to use the house while he was away, but seeing her meek and apologetic attitude, he relents. Still, the feeling of a barrier between them persists, even when they are together in bed.

He urges her to tell him everything that has transpired in his absence. He assures her that even if he does get angry, it will clear the air and melt the obstacle separating them. It is then that Naoko confesses that she has been seduced by her cousin. Kensaku, shocked though he is, realizes immediately that she is not to blame for the act and forgives her. He forgives her in his mind, that is, but he soon realizes that there is something deep within him that cannot forgive so easily.

Grieving over the event that has taken place and also over his inability to put it aside and take up his relationship with his wife as before, Kensaku comes to understand himself better. He sees that within him dwells a despotic egoist that rules tyrannically over him, governing his relationship with others.

This latest misfortune too Kensaku cannot help linking with the circumstances of his birth. He feels himself caught in a swamp, his feet sinking lower and lower into the muck. His good friend Suematsu urges him to try to put the whole matter out of his head, to make his will control his feelings. But this is precisely what he cannot do. "Something has happened that must change the very nature of our relationship as man and wife."

From an external point of view, the days that follow seem peaceful enough. Naoko gets on very well with O-Ei, who has come to live with them. Outwardly Kensaku and Naoko seem to be as intimate as before the incident. But for Kensaku, at least, this is only the outward appearance. At times the consciousness of his wife's seduction acts upon him as a kind of sexual stimulus, which even makes him want to hear from her a detailed account of everything that took place. At other times he feels so dispirited that he does not know what to do with himself. He seeks solace in Naoko's embrace, only to find there something like an iron plate keeping them apart. His health also suffers, and he frequently flies into violent rages at slight provocation. Naoko accepts these tantrums meekly, realizing they are somehow connected with her shame. Her patience but makes him the more violent. He is so changed that even O-Ei cannot believe that this is the old Kensaku.

He takes to visiting the old temples again, sometimes on overnight excursions, and this helps somewhat to return him to his former self. Naoko is pregnant again, and he becomes very gentle to her. He rejoices when his daughter, Takako, is safely delivered.

Still, there remains something within him that will not readmit Naoko to their former intimacy. After an incident in which this subconscious element in him almost results in grave injury to Naoko, she accuses him of telling her that he has forgiven her when he really has not. She cannot help feeling that he hates her and will never be able to forgive her. Thus pressed by Naoko, Kensaku admits: "What you say is true to a degree. That is my problem. My thoughts are generous, my feelings are not. I am an egoist, a pragmatist. I can't help it. I always have been."

It is then that he decides to go away for half a year or so and try to take himself in hand. He will go to Mt. Daisen in Tottori Prefecture, where he will live the life of a monk in a Buddhist temple. He is determined to come back a changed man.

Life on Mt. Daisen turns out to be good medicine for him. He reads the Buddhist scriptures and is deeply moved. But it is nature that has the greatest medicinal effect upon him. Kensaku leisurely reflects upon his life of the past few months and especially upon his attitude toward his wife. In a long letter to her, he writes that he thinks he is about ready to return and take up his life with her again as it was before the incident.

There is still one further stage to full recovery, however, and this very quickly takes place. At one of the temples he meets Take, a man who loves and is deeply considerate of his wife, though she is constantly unfaithful to him. Kensaku reflects that Take knows his wife so perfectly that he can understand why she is as she is, and can therefore forgive her. His own life has been under the influence of the curse of his birth. But, he reflects, if he were another Take, he would be able to transcend such curses, go beyond their power to harm him. He climbs into the mountains. When he is so tired that he can no longer go on, he stops and rests.

A night spent on the mountain results in his falling ill. He runs a high temperature and becomes delirious. In his delirium he calls out again and again for Naoko, and the people at the temple send for her. His illness lasts for many days and there is a possibility that it is cholera. Naoko hurries to the temple. The last passage of the novel describes their meeting. When she enters the room, he asks first about the baby. He places his open hand on her knees and she impulsively takes it. He looks silently into her face. He sees it overflowing with a tender love, such as he has never seen in any other face before. Naoko tries to tell him that everything is all right, but words seem so empty that she remains silent. He tells her that he is feeling fine, that the doctor assures him that there is nothing to be afraid of. The novel ends with the following passage:

Kensaku seemed to be very tired. His hand still in hers, he closed his eyes. There was a deep peace reflected on his face. This was the first time Naoko had ever seen him looking so peaceful. But she was afraid that he would not get well. Strangely enough, though, the thought did not make her sad. She sat there for a long time, looking at his face, feeling drawn to him. "Whether he gets well or not, I will never leave him, I will be with him always," she kept repeating to herself. (VIII, 264)

V   *Process of Composition*

In a postscript written for the first publication of the novel as a whole, Shiga gives considerable information concerning the circumstances of its composition and his aim in writing. The first part, he writes, caused him the greatest difficulty. He began it in 1912 at the age of thirty when he was living in Onomichi, and he took as his subject matter the long-continuing conflict with his father. The difficulty in writing arose in great part from his desire to transcend personal emotion and to write something that would not embarrass his father. After their reconciliation in 1917, his interest in the novel, especially in the theme he had chosen, diminished, all the more since he had already written an objective account of the affair in "A Certain Man and the Death of His Sister."

Then he recalled that one night at the height of the conflict with his father when he had not been able to get to sleep, many thoughts had rushed into his mind, among them the fantasy that he was not his father's son but his grandfather's. He had dismissed the notion for the fantasy that it was, but later when he saw his novel disintegrate for lack of material, he suddenly saw the possibility of restructuring it about this fiction. He would write about the vicissitudes of fortune that might attend a hero born under such infelicitous circumstances, circumstances known to everyone but himself.[2] It was at this point that the novel *Tokito Kensaku* became *Journey Through Dark Night*.

Even then the novel was not easy to write, and he considered doing it as a series of independent sketches, which he could later collect into one volume. In fact, the first section of the novel to see publication was the last chapters of Part II, under the title of "A Man to be Pitied," followed by the novel's prologue, under the title of "Kensaku's Recollections." Finally Parts I, II, and III were serialized in the magazine *Kaizo* between 1921 and 1923, with an occasional break (once as long as five months). Part IV began to appear three years later, in the fall of 1926, and by June of 1928 Shiga had gotten his hero to the top of Mt. Daisen (the end of Chapter 15). It was not until nine years later, in 1937, however, that he was able to complete the concluding five chapters.

Shiga had great love and respect for his grandfather, as we have seen in earlier chapters; therefore he made the grandfather in the novel as different as possible from his real grandfather. Kensaku is, of course, himself. "Kensaku's actions and feelings," he writes, "represent what I myself would do if placed in similar circumstances, or what I would want to do, or what I have actually done" (X, 185). Kensaku's mother appears only in the prologue, but the words and actions ascribed to her were really those of his grandmother. The father in the novel has some of the features of Shiga's father. Shiga tried to make Naoko as unlike his own wife as possible, "but in the course of the writing she gradually grew to be very much like her. . . . Her circumstances, however, are completely fabrications" (X, 186).

The descriptions of the first part were written at the scene or very shortly thereafter. For the description of the mountain scenery of Daisen, Shiga relied upon his recollections of an excursion there some twenty-four years earlier. "Perhaps because the original impression of the scene had been so deep, it came back vividly to mind." (X, 185–86)

VI   *Themes and Motifs*

For my theme I explored the sorrowful effects the almost unblamable peccadillo of a woman could have not only upon herself but also upon those about her. . . . The hero by reason of his mother's act falls under a curse and suffers. Then just as he believes himself to be finally rid of the curse, he falls under it anew through his own wife's seduction. . . . *Journey Through Dark Night* depicts not so much the development of external events as the movement of the hero's spirit by reason of these events, the development that takes place within him. (X, 187)

In the final sentence of the above passage Shiga gives us the key to the theme of the novel. From beginning to end *Journey Through Dark Night* presents the various stages of feeling experienced by the hero in his long struggle to the light. The two seductions, whose effects the author purports to explore, form the central axis of the plot and serve to give a semblance of structure to this long, highly subjective novel, but they are never really of central concern. The focus all the way through is upon the spirit of the hero as he reacts to external events. Moreover, it is not even true to say that the novel depicts the "movement" of the hero's spirit. There is little or no movement depicted; the novel is extremely static. Rather it is the successive stages that are depicted, without showing them as developing from one stage to the next.

In general, four distinct stages of Kensaku's changing consciousness are presented in the course of the novel. The first two, which appear in Parts I and II, alternate rather than succeed each other. They are the stage of confidence in self, in his work, and in the ability of man to prevail over his dark fate; and the stage of depression, of complete spiritual impoverishment, and of deep pessimism concerning his own future and the future of man. In Part III he has found a peace that is only partially disturbed by the death of his infant daughter. In Part IV he is plunged once again into the lower depths because of what happens to his wife, Naoko, but in the end he achieves enlightenment and comes to enjoy a still deeper peace than before.

VII   *Burn Myself Out in a Great Cause*

The first stage appears most strikingly in a long entry Kensaku makes in his journal:

I have the desire to burn myself out in a great cause. But what should I do? What can the dimly burning light in the slender glass chimney hanging from the eaves do, as night sets in, about its desire to conquer the dark? Let the storm come. Let it break the glass. Let it blow the kerosene onto the dry wood of the eaves. Then finally it will become a giant flame. Unless something like that happens to me, I will remain all my life nothing more than a small flame in a glass cage.

I must apply myself much more earnestly to my studies. I feel myself very confined, both in my life and in my work. And I cannot set myself free. I must have much more freedom—so that I can stretch out and do the sort of thing I want to do. I must walk, not with a stagger, but planting each foot firmly on the ground, step after step, swinging my arms, in a pleasant state of mind. Without hurrying, but without stopping to rest. . . .

I do not want to achieve peace by giving up my endeavor at any point. Rather, I want to find a higher peace and satisfaction by pursuing my aim relentlessly, never stopping, never giving up. For a man who has done an immortal work there can be no death. . . .

Man's fate need not be linked to the fate of the earth. I do not know about the other animals. But man at least tries to resist the fate apportioned to him. Behind the inexhaustible instinctive expectation man places in his work must be a blind will making its power felt. Man's mind accepts the inevitability of the extinction of the race, but this blind will absolutely refuses to admit such a possibility. . . .

Behind man's instinctive urge toward progress lies the desire for the long life of the race. In other words, man fights against the fate that has been assigned to him and tries to escape from it. All this is the effect of one tremendous will at work in all men. . . . While we acknowledge the inevitable extinction of the race with our intellects, still in our feelings we are unable to accept such an eventuality. . . . Isn't this because somewhere within us we cling to the hope that we will not be destroyed when the earth meets its end? Isn't this because a tremendous will, somewhere below the level of consciousness, is at work in us? (VIII, 95-99)

Kensaku takes an attitude of confrontation toward everything —other people, nature, fate, man's history—and he is filled with a mighty ambition. As an artist, he is determined to accomplish an immortal work, "a work that will contribute to the happiness of the entire human race, a work that will advance mankind along the direction which it must take" (VII, 222).

This is the attitude of Shiga himself at the high tide of his conflict with his father. It is the attitude already seen in "Otsu Junkichi" and that we will see shortly in "Han's Crime." This part of *Journey Through Dark Night* is undoubtedly the part that was salvaged from the earlier uncompleted work, *Tokito Kensaku*.

VIII   *A Man to be Pitied*

The attitude of confrontation was extremely superficial and was never really able to sink deep roots into Kensaku (Shiga). It was little more than the product of the excited irritation caused by external conflict. It was an attitude easy enough to confide to a journal, but one difficult to realize in daily life. In the very passage quoted above, expressing Kensaku's determination to work for the happiness of the race, it can be seen how much of the bravado is pose, for the passage continues as follows:

He turned these thoughts over in his head, but his spirit had lost its resilience and refused to respond to them. He felt as if he were being sucked further and further down. If the words "Blessed are the poor in spirit" were meant to refer to the present condition of his spirit, they were much too cruel. How could it ever be said that his present spiritual state was all right, that it was blessed? . . . Was there any more pitiable state to be in than this? None of the usual adjectives—lonely, painful, sad—could adequately describe his present feeling. His spirit was immeasurably impoverished. To be so poor in spirit, to have a spirit thus impoverished—could there be any more miserable condition? (VII, 222)

Unlike the attitude of confrontation, this poverty of spirit manifests itself everywhere in Kensaku's actions. He progressively degenerates until he is completely enslaved to his carnal instincts. This process is vividly described in some of the finest passages to come from Shiga's pen. Nakamura Mitsuo points out that never before in Japanese literature—despite the vast amount of writing that is centered on the pleasure quarter—had man's sexual instincts been presented so baldly as a perfectly natural phenomenon not in need of apology. He goes on to state that this is the best book to put into the hands of a young girl preparing for marriage to show her what it is to be a man. At the same time, he adds, no Japanese novel has ever made a more forceful presentation of the dark melancholy that accompanies the kind of profligacy that has as its only object the satisfaction of lust.[3]

The events in Shiga's life that lie behind these passages are his own struggle until marriage with the despotic demands of the flesh and the series of misfortunes that befell him between the years 1912 and 1917, the year of his reconciliation with his father: the continuing discord with his father, further aggravated by his marriage; the grave injury sustained in the streetcar accident; his wife's nervous condition; his continued inability to write; and the death of his first child.

Despite the darkness of Kensaku's experiences of this time, there are already glimmers of the light that harmony with nature will eventually bring. On the boat to Onomichi at the beginning of Part II, for example, he stands on the deck at night and has the feeling that he is

. . . enclosed in some mammoth thing. Above him, below him, before him, behind him, to left and right was infinite darkness. He was standing here in the center of it. People on shore were sound asleep in their homes. He alone stood here face to face with nature. He was the representative of all these others. . . . He was unable to shake off the feeling that he was being swallowed up by this huge thing that surrounded him. It was not necessarily a bad feeling, but he did feel puny and helpless. (VII, 130–31)

Even in his dark excursions to Yoshiwara there is the suggestion that in yielding himself to his sexual instincts, he is in fact yielding himself to nature, trusting that nature in her good time will release him from his bondage. That is why in the very last passage of Part II Kensaku can seem to find spiritual relief in fondling a harlot's breasts:

He tenderly grasped her full and heavy breasts. He felt an indescribable pleasure, as if he held in his hands something of great worth. He shook them lightly and felt their pleasant fullness in his hands. He could not describe his feeling at this moment. He could only exclaim, "A bumper crop! A bumper crop!" as he kept on shaking them. Somehow or other, it seemed to him that they were the symbols of the only thing that mattered, the only thing that could fill his emptiness. (VII, 237)

It is this section of the novel that was the first to be published, under the title of "A Man to be Pitied."

IX Quiet Melancholy

There is only a short time lapse between the end of Part II and the beginning of Part III, but the reader is ushered into an altogether changed world. Kensaku has been in Kyoto for a month and is convalescing from his spiritual illness.

"For the first time he had somewhat the feeling of being saved." The influences of ancient landmarks, ancient temples, and ancient art have a therapeutic effect on him, and he goes "from temple to temple, enjoying the flush of well-being of a convalescent and a feeling of calmness and humility" (VIII, 6). The account of his meeting and marriage with Naoko is presented as a kind of romantic idyl. Their life together is extremely peaceful and pleasant. But even so, Kensaku experiences a strange melancholy and is still unable to write. Soon they are looking forward with joy to the arrival of their first child. The child is safely delivered but dies shortly after birth. Part III ends with the following passage:

Kensaku returned to the writing which he had neglected for some time. He wished to become completely absorbed in it,, but he felt a kind of oppressive fatigue of both body and spirit and was unable to concentrate on his work. All objects about him seemed to have taken on a leprous hue. Everything had paled as after a fainting spell. . . . Why did the world bare its white fangs at him like this? Was this the form that Fate took for him? He would have to think about that. He realized that many before him had lost children. Nor was his child the only one that had ever died after a long, painful struggle. . . . He understood this. Still, after having fought his way along the long, dark road in the hope of reaching light and a new life, and having finally arrived, as he thought, at his destination, to have his first child which was to have been the source of joy become instead the cause of added suffering—he couldn't help discerning in this an invisible malice. Even though he told himself that that was nonsense, the feeling would not leave but took even stronger possession of him. (VIII, 145—46)

In writing this section Shiga was recalling the events and feelings of his early married life, especially of the years 1915 and 1916. Shiga had found peace of a sort, but a peace lined with a deep melancholy. It was the period shortly before his reconciliation with his father, when he had lost the will to assert himself strongly, but had not yet reached a full harmony with nature. The death of his daughter plunged him once again into darkness, but not so deep a darkness as before.

X *Dissolved in Nature*

Kensaku finally concludes his long journey through dark night in the final section of the novel. But before that he is forced, as a result of his wife's misfortune, to experience the darkest trial of all. The first step toward the enlightenment on Mt. Daisen is the realization of his own shortcomings. His friend Suematsu tells him that he is a tyrannical despot, a consummate egoist: "I don't say that you yourself are so, but there is a tyrant living in you, I feel. I suppose one might say that you are the first to suffer at his hands" (VIII, 181).

Kensaku's reaction to this criticism is as follows:

Kensaku realized that until now he had indeed been led about through
the nose by this tyrannical element in himself, but he had not previously
considered it to be his enemy. Now as he recalled many incidents from the
past in which he had forced things to go his own way, he could not but admit to himself that his adversary had indeed been the tyrant dwelling
within him. This was true of the matter with Naoko, too. He had told her to
leave everything to him, that she should stay in the background, that if she
were to show her face she would merely get in the way of solution. He
realized now for the first time that the reason he had said this was that unconsciously he looked for a solution only within himself. Very strange indeed, he reflected. "The struggle with this thing within me will continue to
the end of my life. Then it would have been better if I had never been
born." (VIII, 181–82)

On Mt. Daisen he first loses his apprehension about the fate of
man and his earth and learns to contemplate with equanimity and
resignation the destined extinction of both.

Reflecting upon his past, that had been wasted in trivial intercourse with
men, he felt that a broader world had opened up before him. Looking up at
the graceful figure of a bird gently winging its way high into the blue sky,
he thought of the ugliness of the airplane made by man. Several years
earlier when he had been deeply attached to the work he was doing, he had
had nothing but praise for the indomitable will of man that conquered over
sea, land, and air. But now he had come to the exactly opposite way of feeling. Could it be the will of nature that man should fly like a bird or make
his way through the waters like a fish? The unlimited lust of man, would it
not eventually lead him to disaster? Would not man, in his hubris, eventually receive stern punishment?
   The reason why he had once had so much praise for the limitless ambition of man was that he had felt that this ambition was the unconscious will
that would rescue man from this earth, which was destined for eventual extinction. He had considered everything he saw and heard as but the expression of that unconscious will of man. He had thought that every man who
was really a man must work toward that consummation. It was in this way
that he had interpreted his own excited feeling that came from his attachment to his work.
   But now all that had changed. He was still very much attached to his
work and still got excited over it. But now he felt that he could even rejoice
over the prospective extinction of man and his earth. He didn't know

anything about Buddhism, but he felt a strange attraction toward the state of Nirvana. (VIII, 224)

In the following letter to his wife, Kensaku shows that the process of enlightenment is already under way.

Since coming here, I am much improved and I am at peace with myself. It is good for many reasons that I came here. I spend my days in reading and writing. When it doesn't rain, I take a walk in the mountains and woods or to the river. On this mountain I renew my acquaintance with nature and observe birds, insects, trees, grasses, and stones. When I look at them closely all by myself, I see them in a way I never saw them before and I am filled with joy at observing a world that I never knew existed unfold itself before me . . . and I feel all the things that have been bothering me these past few years pleasantly dissolve. . . . If this feeling really becomes a part of me, I am sure that I will no longer be dangerous to others or to myself. At any rate I have begun to experience the joy that comes from a humble heart. . . . I am overjoyed that this feeling has come over me so naturally and so soon. Until now I couldn't help feeling and acting toward you as I did. It was no good to be sorry for it. But from now on we can be at ease with one another. I don't want you to have to worry any longer about our relationship. . . . In the future I will probably still get angry and say and do things that upset you, but I want you to believe that there will be nothing behind it. . . . When I get off this mountain I do not intend to return to my former self. . . . I know that I have been very stupid. But, like an illness, this thing within me had to go through a process of recovery. Now I have been through it, so there is no longer anything to worry about. (VIII, 235–36)

Finally he achieves the crowning enlightenment on the top of the mountain. The experience is described in the following passage, the climactic passage of the novel:

He was very tired, but his fatigue was at the same time a kind of intoxication. He felt body and spirit melt into nature. It was as if nature enfolded his puny self into its infinite vastness and he was dissolved in it. This was accompanied by a delight impossible to express. He had not a single worry. It was like the nice feeling one has of falling asleep when one is tired. He actually did feel as if he were half asleep. This was not the first time he had experienced the feeling of being dissolved in nature, but the feeling of intoxication was new. His experience until now had been not so much of being dissolved in nature as of being swallowed up by it. At the same time as he had felt a certain sense of well-being, he had experienced as well a certain natural resistance of the will to what was happening. And this resistance of the will had produced a sense of uneasiness. But he felt nothing of this now. He no longer had the slightest wish to resist; he felt only pleasure at dissolving and letting everything take its natural course.

The night was still; the birds of night were not to be heard. Below him hung a thin haze, enough to conceal the lights of the villages. All that was to be seen were the stars and below them the faint outline of the mountain, looking like some large animal. He felt as if he had taken a step forward on the road that led to eternity. He felt not the slightest fear of death. (VIII, 254–55).

XI *Critical Appraisal*

If *Journey Through Dark Night* is judged according to the critical standards ordinarily applied to Western novels, its defects are all too obvious. In the first place, it has—as even its greatest admirers readily admit—but one character, Kensaku. All the other characters are sketched in so lightly that they seem little more than the stage setting for the dramatization of the hero's internal struggle. This is true even of Naoko, who is, in the words of Hasegawa Izumi, "like a doll tossed about on the waves of Kensaku's feelings."[4]

Moreover, apart from the hero's immediate circle of relatives and friends, no external world is allowed to intrude upon his solitude. The time of the action of the novel is that of the First World War, of the rice riots, of the growing disenchantment with capitalism and the rise of proletarian thought, of great social unrest occasioned by wide unemployment, of new currents of writing in reaction to the above. But no hint of any of this finds its way into the novel. The outside world is ignored completely.

A more serious defect is that the hero himself remains largely abstract due to the fact that the reader learns much about his feelings but little about his concrete circumstances, and almost never sees him in action. Contributing to this impression of abstractness is the fact, already mentioned, that the transitional stages between the hero's states of feeling are not well depicted. Nakamura Mitsuo points out:

In the first place, it is not really made clear what the hero does for a living. From certain passages we gather that he is sufficiently well-circumstanced and that he seems to be writing novels. But the only time that his writing appears to constitute the basic rhythm of his life is in the few months he spends at Onomichi. . . . If he really took his writing seriously, it should not occupy such a negligible place in his feelings. . . .

But even granted that he is a writer, he is a writer living in a vacuum where no trace of human society or friends in the same profession is to be found. Even his daily life is lived in a vacuum that is completely lacking in social dimension. Everyone who reads *Journey Through Dark Night* notes that none of the events of the age make their appearance there. But it is more than this. Even the few characters that do enter into relationship with Kensaku in the course of the novel do not seem to impinge upon him with a living force. Rather, they are shadowy figures that enter into the ambit of his life only at his convenience and suddenly vanish when he has no further use for them.

Thus Kensaku is never more than a kind of abstract existence as far as the reader is concerned (despite the fact that the movement of Kensaku's sensibilities is always so immediate). The reason why people do not ordinarily advert to this fact is that the abstraction is in the area of feelings, and most readers firmly believe that the world of feeling is necessarily something concrete.

But to depict a man only in his feelings is clearly a form of abstraction, since it is not feeling alone that accounts for a man's conduct in life. To reduce man to merely feeling is to enclose him in the world of animal, and it is impossible to write a novel with an animal as hero. Then why was it possible . . . for *Journey Through Dark Night* to achieve the impossible? It was because the readers of that day saw behind the abstract hero the figure of the writer himself. It was because the readers accepted the novel unconditionally as an autobiographical novel presenting the idealized self of the author.[5]

The drama of Kensaku's journey through dark night, then, is an internal one. Real interaction with other people is lacking throughout the novel. Some critics, however, make much of the fact that at the end, finally, for one brief moment, Naoko comes alive and Kensaku looks upon her with new eyes. Edwin McClellan thinks that here for the first time Kensaku comes to have understanding and respect for another and thus is finally able to enter into his true self. In McClellan's interpretation, Shiga is making "the simple yet profound statement . . . that it is through discovering objective reality outside of oneself and coming to terms with it that one can come to terms with oneself." When Kensaku eats spoiled fish and becomes ill, it is not only the poison in his stomach that he rejects, but also the poison in his soul. His illness is a complete catharsis. At the end he receives his wife with love, and in a silence like death there is the powerful affirmation of human dignity. "And death, even if it should come to Kensaku, seems not to matter in the face of this affirmation."[6] This, McClellan asserts, gives the novel a moral context and the power to move us.

A Western reader is very much tempted to read this final scene in this way, especially since it is an axiom of modern psychology that self-definition cannot take place in isolation from others. But this is not, we think, the correct reading. The novel has an Eastern conclusion, not a Western. It is in the depths of his own psyche that Kensaku reaches the resolution to his problems. He goes to Mt. Daisen to get over the repulsion he feels toward his wife because of what has happened to her. He does indeed get over it, but not in such a way that he can go down from the mountain and take up his daily life with her again. What he discovers on Mt. Daisen is that nothing in the world of men really matters. All men, he himself included, are part of nature; the boundaries that have served to distinguish self from other, whether human or nonhuman, have melted away, and he has the strong feeling of having been purified in body and spirit. Let death come, he is ready for it. He has transcended the distinction between life and death. By the same token he has transcended the boundaries of human relationships. There may be love in his eyes as he looks upon Naoko, but it is the look that he bestows now upon all of nature, a look that can no longer distinguish between human and nonhuman. Shiga leaves his hero poised between life and death, not caring which it will be; and he assimilates Naoko to Kensaku's state of feeling. She understands that he may not recover. "Strangely enough, though, this thought did not really make her sad." The reader may well ask: "Why shouldn't this thought make her sad?" The answer is obvious. It is not Naoko's consciousness that we are being shown here, but Kensaku's still. He may wear the mask of Naoko but there is no mistaking his identity.

Kamei Katsuichiro also points out that in this last scene there is no question of any kind of conversion on the part of Kensaku. There is only the action of nature upon him. He covers over his wife's "fault" with the heart of nature, and the condition that made this possible was the very real possibility of death. "It is not a question of the happiness of family. There is merely a light which nature suddenly bestows upon him—a light which he had not expected and which indeed came to him only with the approach of death."[7] Sudo Matsuo also asserts that just as Shiga's original experience on Mt. Daisen was an experience in isolation, so the literary reconstruction of the same experience at the end of *Journey Through Dark Night* is the experience of one alone, Kensaku. There could be no question here of the discovery of another person or of a reconciliation with other men. "It was difficult," Sudo states, "for Shiga to take the world of Daisen, which had been essentially a matter of his own solitary experience, and write into it another character besides Kensaku."[8] In real life the Daisen experience had been for him only a point of enlightenment, not a solution or a conclusion. It was the world of one person, not the realization of reconciliation. Therefore it could not very well effect a reconciliation between Kensaku and Naoko. The reader is moved by the scene, but it is neither a conclusion nor a resolution.

XII   Journey Through Dark Night *as a Lyrical Novel*

Journey Through Dark Night can best be read as a lyrical novel. Tanikawa Tetsuzo, one of Shiga's greatest admirers, admits that from the point of view of the Western novel, this work cannot be thought of as a novel. It is more like a picture scroll (*e-maki*) that unfolds one frame at a time.[9] Edward Seidensticker suggests that it be read as a kind of *uta-monogatari*, such as *The Tales of Ise*, a sequence of poetic flights held together by the cement of prose.[10]

Certainly it helps to think of the novel in this way. There is much to please us in individual parts, and in lyrical writing we do not expect to find much development, interaction, and cause and effect. Many of the parts of *Journey Through Dark Night* are excellent when taken as lyrical statement. No writer is more skillful than Shiga in interweaving nature with the moods of the hero. Moreover nature is always something concrete, the nature of a particular place at a particular season of the year. His nature is so localized that Japanese readers claim to be able to recognize the scene at once. In this novel we also find the same spare style we find in his best short stories. In a few words he is able to evoke a mood or describe a place or situation.

But the fact remains that in *Journey Through Dark Night* Shiga was making use of material that required dramatic development as well as lyrical, and this was not given it. Shiga, after all, does pose basic problems of human relationships—especially that between man and wife, of the meaning of life and death, of the effects of sin and human error. After having been presented with such weighty problems, how can the reader be content with Shiga's final answer: "Forget about these problems, live sincerely, be faithful to self, entrust yourself to nature and live with her in full harmony"?

CHAPTER 5

A Golden Ten

M OST of the stories we have considered to this point, as well as the one novel, have been very close to autobiography and have lacked, in greater or lesser degree, the kind of structural form that we expect to find in good fiction. Individual passages have been excellent, but too often they have stood out brightly against a dreary backdrop. Some of the stories have been of no literary interest whatsoever and were considered only because of what they told us about the author.

Shiga was hampered by a literary theory that inhibited the writing of fiction, but he could, when he wished, turn out a well-made story with an exemplary unity of structure. The unifying principle might be plot or character or even atmosphere or mood, but every element, every separate part of the story, was tailored to create this unity. In the present chapter we will consider what we judge to be the best of these stories. Western readers and critics, while generally critical of his autobiographical works, have found these short stories of Shiga's more to their liking and have singled out several for particular praise, especially "Han's Crime" and "Seibei's Gourds."

In general we will take up these stories in the order of their writing, since several of them are objective crystallizations of experiences that Shiga treats more subjectively in the works already considered.

I "The Old Man" (1911)

Shiga calls "The Old Man" an exercise in form, interesting and successful only as such. The inspiration for it came from a story by Bjørnstjerne Bjørnson (whose title he later forgot) in which the three most important events of one man's life—his baptism, marriage, and death and burial—are described by a priest who

assisted at all three. "These three points of his life were simply
described, but in such a way that the entire life of the man was
made strangely palpable. I thought it extremely well done" (X,
171).

The old man, who is never named, is a successful businessman
who loses his wife when he is fifty-four and his two children are
already grown. With her death he suddenly seems years older. But
several months later he marries again, a lady one year younger than
his daughter. She so rejuvenates him that he appears to be even
younger than before and plunges into a round of youthful activities.
He starts going to Sumo matches again, takes his wife to plays, and
even goes to enjoy the waters of a mountain spa.

Two years later he retires from his company and becomes adviser
to an oil firm, but leaves this too when the recommendations of a
young engineer, two years behind his son in college, are accepted in
preference to his. He is now sixty-five.

Since his second wife is childless, they adopt the daughter of his
son and lavish affection upon her. After leaving the oil firm he
spends his time building and tearing down houses, at great financial
loss—which, however, he can well afford. His wife dies of tuber-
culosis and he returns their adopted child to her real parents. Now
at sixty-nine he is alone again and lonely.

He takes to frequenting geisha houses and finally sets up one of
the youngest girls, the same age as his oldest granddaughter, as his
mistress, in a house he has built for her and which he promises to
turn over to her completely after three years. They live very happily
together. He is not disturbed by the fact that she has a young lover,
and he feels no jealousy or resentment when she gives birth to her
lover's child. At the end of the contracted three years the mistress
herself proposes another year's extension, and when this year too
passes, a second extension. He is pleased to the point of tears. This
year she gives birth to her lover's second child. When he proposes
still another year's extension, she gladly consents. He now feels
ready for death and prays that it will come quickly, and it does. He
catches cold and this develops into influenza. She joins the family
circle of children and grandchildren at his deathbed, doing what
she can to nurse him. He dies a peaceful death at the age of
seventy-five. In his will he leaves her enough property to enable her
to raise her two children.

Four months later, on the cushion where the old man formerly sat, now sits the young father of her children. In the alcove behind him is a large portrait of the old man, sitting ceremoniously in his formal dress.

Whatever Shiga may have thought of "The Old Man," it is certainly more than an exercise in form. This picture of an old man gradually coming to terms with old age and death is permeated with a warm humanity that elevates the story to a level of universal significance. Though the subject invites sentimentality, Shiga's spare style is always well in control; the story never becomes sentimental.

The pathos of growing old is presented through the skillfully selected details. The sad frustration that a man who is still active experiences upon retirement, for example, is felt in the old man's frenzied building and rebuilding of houses with no prospect of financial gain. When he decides to set up a geisha, he recalls a story he heard in his youth of a certain geisha, who, given the choice between a patron forty-five years old and one seventy-two, chose the latter since he would not be around so long. Hearing the story, he had pitied the old man from his heart. Now he finds himself in that same position and he marvels at the rapid passage of the years.

In the new house with his mistress, surrounded by all new furniture, he feels as if he were still in his twenties or thirties. Yet when he sits across from her and observes her soft, well-fleshed hands, he does not dare let her see his own wizened hands, mere bones covered over with dry skin. He grieves that his arms no longer have the strength to enclose her in a powerful embrace, and that an old man's spirit does not grow old with the rest of him.

Transcending the pathos, however, is a sense of mature ripeness, a feeling that ripeness is all. The man in his old age has grown gentle and understanding—witness the attitude he takes toward his mistress's lover and their children. He has grown to understand and be considerate of others. Shiga gives us sufficient view of him as he was in the past to let it be seen that he was not always this way. Finally, his death at the end gives the impression of completeness and fulfillment rather than of tragedy.

It is remarkable that Shiga, still a young man, should have had such a profound understanding of an old man's psychology; and it is regrettable that he regarded this kind of story as a mere exercise in composition, somehow outside the range of his proper talent.

The central theme of "The Old Man" is the central theme of most of Shiga's work—that nature is best, that one should entrust oneself to its processes, finding there rest and contentment. The reason the old man's death is not tragic is that it is the culmination of a natural process to which he, at the end at least, has committed himself entirely.

II "The Razor" (1910)

"The Razor" is the product of the same morbid imagination that was found at work in "Confused Head," published five months later, and in "For Grandmother," which came out the following year. Shiga states that the starting point for this story was the feeling of threat everyone experiences in the barber's chair. But it is probably more exact to say that the story originated in the feeling of threat that he himself experienced in his unsettled life at this time.

"The Razor" is a study in mood and atmosphere. What could possibly drive a respectable barber, who has probably never injured anyone in his life before, to sink his razor into the throat of an unsuspecting client? The excellence of the story lies in the high degree of plausibility the author is able to lend to this action.

Yoshisaburo is a young barber who has inherited his barber shop by marrying the daughter of its former proprietor, who has since died. As the story begins, he is in bed with a bad cold just before a holiday when he can expect many clients to come in. His two skilled assistants have just left him, and their replacements are not dependable. As he burns with fever in his bed, everything he sees and hears contributes to a growing impatience and sense of frustration. The very room in which he lies seems sick with fever. The anxious solicitude of his well-intentioned wife but makes him the more fretful. Rising from his bed, he hones and strops a razor that has been brought to him for sharpening; but its owner soon returns to report that it still will not cut, and he has a second try at it.

After he had honed the blade, he began to strop it. It seemed as if the stagnant air of the room were set in motion by the sound of the razor against the strop. Yoshisaburo was able to control his shaking hand, and to strop with some kind of rhythm. But still it did not go well. Then the nail which his wife had pounded into the pillar suddenly fell out. The strop came flying down and wrapped itself several times around the blade. (I, 138–39)

He takes the razor out to the shop and continues working on it. The last client has left when a young man of twenty-two or so rushes in and asks for a shave. Though he is dressed in a new kimono and appears to be very conceited, Yoshisaburo can tell immediately that he is only a day laborer putting on airs. Yoshisaburo is all the more disgusted when he learns that the man is on his way to a brothel.

Yoshisaburo begins to shave him. But the blade will not cut properly, his hand is shaking, and his nose has begun to run. Inside the house the baby is crying. Yoshisaburo is further irritated by the insensitivity of his client: he sits there composed while the dull razor scrapes painfully over his skin. The barber does his best to give him a clean shave, but with little success. He becomes first angry, then discouraged.

He felt like breaking down and crying. Body and spirit were completely worn out. His fever-swollen eyes were moist and felt as if they were about to melt away of fever.

He did the throat, then the cheeks, then the chin, then the forehead, then back to the soft portion of the throat. This last part, no matter how carefully he worked, he could not do as he wished. He scraped and scraped, but with little effect. His patience was near the breaking point; an urge came over him to pare it off, skin and all. He looked at the face before him with its rough-grained skin, pores filled with grease, and the urge became all the stronger. The young man in the meantime had fallen asleep. His head was swung back, his mouth wide open, revealing a set of ill-matched dirty teeth.

Yoshisaburo was so tired that he could hardly stand. He felt as if poison had been poured into every joint. He wanted to stop and lie down. Enough! This was enough! So he decided again and again. But with the force of inertia, he kept on his struggle with each individual stubborn hair. (I, 141–42)

At this point the blade chances to cut into the flesh. Yoshisaburo feels all his lethargy and fatigue suddenly depart. As he watches, the skin where the blade has entered changes from a milky white to a pale crimson until finally red blood rises to the surface. A globule of dark red blood swells and then breaks, and the blood falls away in a trickle. At this point Yoshisaburo is seized by a kind of frenzy.

The frenzy took a very strong hold of him. His breath became shorter and shorter. It seemed as if all of him, body and spirit, were being sucked into that wound. Try as he would, he could no longer control the impulse. He regripped the razor so that the tip pointed downward and with lightning speed plunged it into the throat until the blade was completely embedded in flesh. The young man did not so much as shudder.

Yoshisaburo, almost in a faint, fell into the chair beside him. His tautness suddenly relaxed. But the heavy fatigue returned and he fell asleep, a deep, deathlike sleep. The night too was deathly still. All movement had come to a stop; everything was fallen into a deep sleep. The mirror alone, from three different angles, coldly surveyed the scene. (I, 142—43)

"The Razor," as mentioned above, has the aim of making this highly unlikely murder seem plausible. With a selection of detail characteristic of Shiga at his best, everything in the story builds up to this climax and makes it seem inevitable. There is no other statement and only the minimum of characterization needed to achieve the effect. Though lacking in depth, the story is a triumph of craftsmanship.

III   "My Mother's Death and the Coming of My New Mother"
(1912)

This is one of the finest pieces Shiga ever wrote, one in which his celebrated style appears to greatest advantage. The story is divided into seven sections. The first four record the events revolving about the death of Shiga's mother on August 30, 1895.

In the summer of his thirteenth year, Shiga was in summer camp at the sea when he received a letter from his grandfather telling him that his mother was going to have another child. He was so pleased at the news that he spent all of his pocket money to buy a set of shell combs and hairpin to give her as a kind of "reward." When he gets home, his mother is not feeling well and in the weeks that follow she goes from bad to worse and finally dies, the baby with her.

The last three sections tell of the coming of his new mother. Two months after the death of his mother, Shiga's father begins to look around for a new wife. His grandmother shows him a picture of one of the women under consideration and asks his opinion. She is pleasantly surprised at his answer: "Fine as long as she has a good heart." The match is soon arranged, and Shiga waits eagerly for the coming of his new mother, who is very young and much more beautiful than his real mother.

Soon it is the day of the wedding, and Shiga awkwardly takes his part in the ceremonies. He even does a traditional dance at the reception that follows. He is disgusted when his father, who has had too much to drink, tells one of the geisha present that she is the loveliest woman in the room.

The next day the boy self-consciously goes through his morning routine of washing and dressing, and then goes to greet his new mother. He is filled with joy as he speaks to her alone for the first time. That night, after he has already gone to bed, his father sends a maid to ask if he wouldn't like to sleep beside his mother. He goes to their room. His father is in an unusually fine mood and keeps repeating that "after all, children are a man's greatest treasure." After his father has gone to sleep, he talks with his mother for a while and then goes back to sleep with his grandparents. His grandmother questions him about the conversation in the other room, but he pretends to be asleep and lies there quietly relishing a feeling of deep joy.

In the days that follow he is pleased that everyone is all praise for his new mother, and his real mother's death recedes quickly into the past. He accompanies his mother and grandmother on their rounds of the relatives, and feels a gentle pride when he sees men turn in the street to take a second look as they pass. In the years that follow, his mother gives birth to a boy and three girls.

Of the composition of this story, Shiga writes:

I wrote of the events of my childhood exactly as they had taken place. I was able to finish this piece in one night. The boy that appears here is certainly sentimental, but the writing is not, a fact that greatly pleased me. Whenever I am asked to name a favorite among my writings, I often pick this one. If stories that have been completed only after great labor usually display a perfection proportionate to the pain that gave them birth, there is another perfection to be found in those that have flowed effortlessly from the author's pen. It appears that the writer is often fonder of the latter. (X, 171—72)

The reader will agree that the writing is not sentimental, and he too may very well select this story as one of his favorites. Here are to be found the elements of Shiga's most accomplished style: feeling that is deep and immediate, but conveyed indirectly through well-chiseled dialogue and masterful selection of detail; expression that is economical, precise, rich in nuance and suggestion.

Two parallel scenes will serve as illustration. The first is that of the morning after his real mother's death, and the second, the morning after his new mother's arrival.

The night before his mother's death Shiga had sat in her room with his father, his grandparents, his great-grandmother, his uncle, and the doctor, watching her breathing grow less and less frequent until it stopped altogether. The account of the following morning begins as follows:

The next morning when I went to light an incense stick, there was no one in the room. I silently lifted the white cloth covering her face and looked at her. I was surprised to see around her mouth a kind of froth, such as one sometimes sees on the mouth of a crab. "She's still alive!" I thought, and I ran to the veranda to tell my grandmother.

My grandmother came and looked. "It's just the air coming out," she explained, wiping the lips gently with a piece of paper.

I put all the shell jewelry I had bought for her at Enoshima into her coffin.

The sound of the hammer nailing down the coffin lid was almost too painful to bear.

They lowered the coffin into the hole, and I thought, "It's all over!" The thud of clods of clay thrown down on the coffin echoed in my heart.

"Okay?" asked the man who had been standing by impatiently with shovel and hoe, and without so much as a nod to us, he began noisily to fill in the hole. "Even if she did come back to life, she'd never be able to get out," I thought. (I, 259—60)

Though Shiga never tells us that he was grief-stricken at his mother's death, his sorrow is made powerfully present by the details he selects as significant. The time covered in this brief passage is considerable (presumably his mother was not buried the day after her death), but with a few well-executed strokes of the pen he is able to intimate the whole complex of grief from death to burial of one who has seen a loved one depart this world. This prose has the texture and concentration of poetry.

With the same economy of detail is portrayed the thirteen-year-old boy's pleasure at meeting his mother for the first time in his home. The previous passage was a description of the wedding ceremony and reception. The next section begins:

The next morning when I got up, my mother was already puttering around the house. I washed my face at the washstand on the veranda, but I could not bring myself to blow my nose in my hand as I usually did.

After I had washed my face, I got the handkerchief [that he had been asked to give her] and went to look for her. She was doing something in the dark room next to the parlor. I handed the handkerchief to her, stammering an explanation.

"Thank you," answered my beautiful mother, looking at me affectionately. This was the first chance we had had to speak to each other alone.

After I had given her the handkerchief, I hopped on one leg down the veranda to the student's room, not that I had any reason to go there. (I, 262)

In this passage too there is no need for him to tell us how he felt. His actions reveal this better than words could.

The parallelism of these two passages, one revealing the boy's great sorrow and the other his equally great joy, is part of the thematic structure of this well-made story, which has for its basic theme the rhythm of nature with its elemental waves of joy and sorrow, life and death. The structure is very well suited to the theme, since it too follows a wave pattern, moving from joy-life to sorrow-death to joy-life again and ending with the suggestion of sorrow-death to come. Section 1 begins on a crest of joy-life, as the boy joyfully anticipates the birth of a brother or sister. From Section 2, in which his mother has become ill, to Section 3, in which she dies, and Section 4, in which she is buried, the wave descends into a trough of death and sorrow. With Section 5, in which is made the arrangement for the new marriage, the wave begins to rise again, through the wedding scene in Section 6, to the crest in Section 7, in which the new mother enters the home and in the years that follow gives birth to a boy and three girls. At the conclusion the wave is already receding. The boy's mother tells him that this last childbirth has been the hardest. He answers, "Now that you are growing older, your constitution is not as strong as it used to be," thinking as he speaks that even his mother, who had once been so young and beautiful, had already arrived at the stage of life where this could be said.

Life, this story suggests, consists basically in this ever-continuing alternation of moments of life and moments of death. Shiga entrusts himself to this natural rhythm, floating along with the tide, ready to accept whatever it will bring, whether sorrow or joy, life or death. This is especially evident in the rapid transition from sorrow at his real mother's death to joy at the coming of his new mother, a transition that is accomplished in the following brief passage:

[My mother's death] was, after all, the first irrevocable event in my life. My grandmother and I often wept together in the bath. But before a hundred days had passed, I was already looking forward with joyful anticipation to the coming of my new mother. (I, 261)

Another short piece written in the same year, "Recollections of My Mother's Death and of her Tabi,"[1] elaborates further upon Shiga's feelings of sorrow and regret at the death of his mother. It begins with a brief account of his mother's death and the events leading up to it, in much the same words as the earlier story, and then goes on to recall an incident that took place about a year or so before her death, an incident which had caused her great pain.

One evening his mother comes to the room where he is working and tries to hand him his *tabi*. Absorbed in what he is doing, he ignores her. Since she is busy with her own work, she does not wait, but puts the *tabi* on his head and walks out. He gets angry and runs after her, shouting loudly his annoyance. She is taken aback at his outburst and gazes at him sadly. Even then he does not desist. The piece ends as follows:

Long afterward I heard from my father that I was often the cause of my mother's weeping. She complained to him that because of my grandmother's overindulgent love, I was so spoiled that she could do nothing with me. According to that, I seem to have given her much grief. But I remember nothing of it. Only this little incident of the *tabi* remains in my memory. I tried to imagine what my mother must have felt. She must have been very sad.

It was only a little out of my way to return from school by way of Aoyama Cemetery. So I occasionally stopped to visit her grave. And I often recalled the *tabi* incident. Each time I bowed to the grave and apologized to her in my heart. (I, 267)

The grief Shiga felt at his mother's death is powerfully presented in the image of the schoolboy bowed in apology before her grave. The tragedy of a boy so young losing his mother is deepened first of all by the feelings of regret for having hurt her so often, and then by the painful realization that of so many incidents that must have occurred, this one of the *tabi* is the only one he can remember.

IV "The Just Ones" (1912)

Both "The Just Ones" and "An Incident," published a year later, tell of a child hit by a streetcar and of the consequences of the accident. Shiga himself points out the difference between the two stories:

> "The Just Ones" takes as its theme the inflated pride of three men who have done what they thought was right and just, and the sad dissatisfaction that overtakes them when their justice is not rewarded. "An Incident" has a more direct feeling. It depicts the joy felt when a child, hit by a streetcar, emerges unharmed. (X, 172)

Three laborers working on the streetcar tracks in the Nihonbashi section of Tokyo are suddenly startled by a woman's cry and look up from their work in time to see a streetcar pressing down upon a little girl walking in the middle of the tracks, her back to it. Only after he has hit the child does the driver remember to apply his emergency brake, which brings the car to an immediate stop. Too late. The child is dead.

A crowd quickly gathers. The police arrive on the scene, also the streetcar-line supervisor. The latter prompts the driver and the conductor to say that the girl had rushed out in front of the streetcar so suddenly that there was not time to apply the emergency brake. Not so, cry out the three workmen, after a hurried consultation. There was plenty of time to apply the brake. The driver lost his presence of mind.

The three workers go along to the police station to present their eyewitness testimony. The supervisor tries to get them to change their story, reminding them that they work for the same company. Despite the implied threat to their jobs, however, they become only the more insistent.

Upon leaving the police station hours later, they experience a strange exhilaration, a pleasant excitement. They walk aimlessly about town, rehearsing among themselves the details of the incident. In their feeling of pride and achievement, they are tempted to stop passersby and ask, "Don't you recognize us?" "Wrong is always wrong," they assure each other. "We only did what we had to do." "The nerve of that guy—expecting that just because we work for the streetcar company we would go along with his story." They are immensely pleased with themselves and expect that their virtue will be rewarded.

But the reward is not forthcoming. The streets are no different from before; their virtue goes unrecognized. As they walk on, they begin to feel let down. A passing ricksha coolie yells at them to get out of the way, and they resent the insult to their dignity. Their pleasantly high spirits slowly ebb away and are replaced by a growing sense of irritation.

They find themselves again at the site of the accident, but no sign of it remains. This seems strange. They feel somehow deprived and angry, as if an injustice has been done them. The policeman in the police box is a young rookie who, of course, was not on duty at the time of the accident. To make matters worse, he glares at them suspiciously.

Only then does the realization hit them that they may now be out of jobs. The youngest of the three thinks of his aged grandmother waiting for him in their gloomy house. Their spirits grow more and more unsettled, and they decide to go somewhere for a drink.

They make their way to the second floor of a café where a number of people are eating and drinking. They still cannot leave the topic, and self-consciously begin discussing it again in voices loud enough to be overheard. Customers and waitresses gather around them to hear the details.

The story by now has become greatly exaggerated. The girl's head and arms were smashed to bloody pulp. The mother went berserk with grief. Their audience reacts with appropriate expressions of horror and concern. Drinking all the while, the workers go on to give a detailed account of the police interrogation, and speculate on what the morning paper will have to say about the incident. By now everyone in the place has stopped his own conversation to listen to them. For the first time since leaving the police station they experience a measure of real satisfaction.

But this does not last long. Their auditors begin to drift away until the three are left to themselves. Although it is already midnight, they keep on drinking, growing dissatisfied and angry as before. The realization that they will be fired from their jobs is now uppermost in their minds. One of the three goes home and the other two, after a few more drinks, decide to go to a brothel. In their separate rickshas each recounts the incident once again to the driver. Their loud, drunken voices echo loudly in the silent streets. The rickshas reach the place of the accident. The older man would stop and have still another look, but the younger urges the drivers on.

Shiga in this story shows a deep knowledge of human nature and profound psychological insight. There is perhaps no one who has not experienced a like exhilaration at a good action performed and subsequent disappointment when tangible reward is not immediately forthcoming, and finally horror when he realizes the dread consequences which in his brash goodwill he had not stopped to take into account.

In this story too every detail is just right in achieving the desired effect and nothing is superfluous. So exactly is the focus of the story on the reaction of the three men that the reader is not even told the results of the police investigation. He never learns if the driver and the streetcar company are held responsible for the accident.

Shiga's skill in presenting scenes of great emotion without lapsing into sentimentality is again seen in his skillful description of the mother's grief:

> The young mother turned pale and lifted her eyes heavenward. She was unable to speak. She approached her daughter once, but then took her stand a short distance away and looked upon the scene as if completely detached from it. Even when the policemen pulled the small, blood-covered body from under the streetcar, she watched them with an eerie coldness as if she were looking at something distant and unconnected with her. Occasionally her empty and lusterless eyes looked sadly and nervously beyond the crowd in the direction of her home in the distance. (II, 78—79)

V "An Incident" (1913)

Shiga tells this story in the first person. He professes it to be an almost exact account of an accident that he himself was witness to. But, as we shall see, it is not the accident itself that is of central interest in the story.

It is a hot, humid, breezeless afternoon in late July. Shiga sits at the front of a streetcar which rumbles along with monotonous rhythm down the nearly deserted street. The heat is so stifling that he has not even the energy to look at the magazine in his hand. With him in the car and also suffering from the heat are a young man with the insignia of an electric company on his cap, and a stern and forbidding expression on his face as he sits half asleep; two students sitting with their legs spread far apart, their bare feet black with grime and sweat—an unpleasant sight to behold; a large man of over forty, perhaps a petty official of some kind or a junior clerk, dressed in a Western suit with a dirty imitation-Panama hat pushed to the back of his head, chin resting on his stick and eyes staring vacantly ahead. A fat woman of about forty, with a red, sweaty face, boards the car. In one hand she carries a parasol; with the other she is wiping the sweat from her throat with a moist towel. Some of the passengers look up at her listlessly, but the others continue in their drowsy, disinterested state. The passengers are too overcome by the heat to pay any attention to each other. Burdened each with his private cares, they sit there insentient, as if they have forgotten where they are going and for what purpose.

A butterfly flies in through the window and flutters about the car for a while, giving the author a momentary sense of relief. It comes to rest on an advertisement for a play and looks very beautiful there.

The author is startled from his reverie by the cry of the driver, and he raises his head in time to see a little boy about to cross the street in the path of the streetcar. The boy is running at full speed, unaware of his danger. The driver applies his brake and the streetcar slows down. Even so, the boy and the streetcar are on a collision course. As the author looks on, the boy disappears under the windshield and there is a thud. The streetcar moves ahead a few more feet, then comes to a stop. The author has a moment of severe shock, followed by a feeling of tremendous relief and joy when he hears the boy sobbing loudly.

In no time a crowd gathers. The young man from the electric company takes the boy in his arms and scolds him roundly. The boy, still crying loudly, tries to get out of his embrace and begins to pummel him with his tiny fists. The other passengers try to console the boy, and they examine him for injuries. Fortunately, the front guard of the streetcar has saved him from being hurt: he has not a single scratch. Someone points out that the boy has wet his pants, and everyone bursts out laughing. The laugh becomes still louder when they see that the young man from the electric company is also wet where the boy has pressed against him. The young man, in retaliation, taps the boy a couple of times on the head with his chin, and the boy begins to sob again.

The mother arrives on the scene. She is over forty, dark-skinned, and ugly. She takes the boy from the young man, gives him a ferocious stare, then slaps him several times. He cries still louder. She draws him to her and shakes him severely. At this point the young man steps forward and tells her that she is the one that is really to blame, and they have an exchange of words.

The story ends as follows:

The clerk, standing somewhat apart from the others, began to walk about in excitement, muttering to himself. Then seeing that the driver had already returned to his seat, he stood in front of him on the street and said, "Good thing it worked," tapping the front guard of the streetcar with his cane. "It couldn't have worked better. This must be the first time since those guards came into use that such a thing has happened." These words were still not sufficient to give adequate expression to his pleasurable feeling of excitement. He seemed to want to say more, but the right words would not come. Besides, the driver was unresponsive.

By this time the crowd had largely dispersed. Most of the people had returned to their houses and were looking on from there. The mother was thanking the conductor profusely. The child, mouth and nose buried in the mother's large breasts, which hung down in an unsightly manner, was now still.

The young man and the clerk reboarded the car. The mother picked up the boy's clogs and started for home. The streetcar began to move again.

The young man removed his jacket and then his shirt, which was wet with urine, exposing his light skin and well-fleshed shoulders. He crumpled the shirt where it was wet and energetically began to wipe his stomach. It was pleasant to watch the rippling movement of his arm and chest muscles. He suddenly lifted his head and met my gaze. (I was sitting across from him.)

"He really fixed me," he said, laughing. The excited and forbidding expression he had previously worn had vanished from his face, and his countenance was now pleasant, good-natured, and sparklingly alive.

At the back of the streetcar the fat woman of about forty was talking to the clerk, who made reply with great earnestness and many gestures. The two students had also begun to converse. The passengers, who before the accident had been half asleep, overcome by the heat, now all had lively expressions on their faces. I too was enjoying a pleasant feeling of exhilaration. Suddenly I noticed that the innocent butterfly, which had fastened itself to the play advertisement, had taken its departure. (II, 110—11)

Most significant in the story is the contrast between the atmosphere in the streetcar before the accident and after. At the beginning is felt the heat, the humidity, the lethargy, the monotony, the general oppressiveness of the day. The passengers, of course, experience all this, but even nature seems to feel it. The streets are deserted. The leaves of the fig trees are dried and curled in, and covered with dust. The streetcar tracks stretch out ahead like two streams of mercury. The streetcar itself rumbles along in monotonous rhythm. But when the streetcar gets under way again after the accident, the passengers have forgotten the heat and everything accompanying it. They sit chatting vivaciously, with lively expressions on their faces, and the author too is "enjoying a pleasant feeling of exhilaration."

The contrast is more than one of atmosphere. The passengers, as a result of the accident, become human. At the beginning they occupy each his own isolated world. That this isolation is something ugly can be seen from the unfavorable impression each makes upon the author.

It is concern for the child that first brings out their humanity. When the streetcar comes to a sudden stop, the first one to stir into action from his lethargy is the young man from the electric company. He rushes out and grabs the child. The others follow him, and each one, except for the author who remains an onlooker throughout, plays his role in ministering to the boy. They feel a common relief in ascertaining that he is unharmed. This relief is intensified into the even deeper feeling of a common humanity when they discover that he has wet himself and the young man. The author calls the laugh that follows this discovery "a laugh of relief." It is the signal that completes the passengers' transformation into "brothers." When they return to the car, they look at each other with fresh eyes, and experience a bond of comradeship. They are now able to converse with each other congenially, and even the author, who has remained most distant from the action, is changed. The earlier unpleasant impression of his fellow passengers has disappeared.

Thus, the theme of this deceptively simple story is nothing less than the rediscovery of common brotherhood and of the innate goodness of man, and the joy at being given fresh evidence of it. Shiga implies as much when he states that he was moved to write this story when he saw the joy of these good-natured people at the child's escape from death.

"An Incident," therefore, is not a simple, artless account of an accident that the author was witness to. Short as it is, it is a fine piece of art. To say and imply so much in so few words is beyond the power of all but the finest writers. This story too is an example of Shiga's style at its best.

We cannot leave this piece without pointing out that the Shiga Naoya that appears in a work such as this is quite a different person from the self-centered monster of "Otsu Junkichi" and his other autobiographical stories. The side of Shiga that appears in "An Incident"—warmhearted, concerned with others, appreciative of the humanity of man wherever it is to be found—too seldom appears in the latter. One wonders if it was not an overscrupulous honesty, a fear of painting himself the least bit better than he actually was, that is responsible for the dreary picture of him that emerges in his other work. Where most autobiographical writers tend to use their works as a kind of apology for self, Shiga Naoya seems to have done just the opposite.

VI   "Claudius's Journal" (1912)

"Claudius's Journal" was inspired by a particularly inept performance of the role of Hamlet in a Japanese production of the play that Shiga went to see. So bad was the actor who played Hamlet that Shiga found himself sympathizing rather with Claudius. What finally moved him to write the story was the discovery that no proof of Claudius's guilt is offered in the play other than the dubious word of the ghost.[2] Before beginning to write, Shiga made a careful study of Tsubouchi's translation of *Hamlet* to make certain that his story would be consistent at every point with the play.

In Shiga's version, Claudius is a very sensitive and good man who has loved Gertrude from before her marriage to his brother. At the

start he has a warm feeling also for her son and wishes nothing more
than to win his understanding and his love. Claudius's only fault is
marrying too soon after his brother's death, thereby inviting mis-
understanding and criticism.

Claudius sees Hamlet's attitude toward him change suddenly
(the day after the ghost's appearance) from resentment to hatred.
He cannot accept Polonius's view that Ophelia is responsible for the
change. He doesn't want to hate Hamlet, if only for the sake of his
wife. He recognizes Hamlet's great talent and fine character.
Perhaps, he thinks, the players will be able to divert him from his
grief.

Claudius realizes that he is so sensitive to criticism that even
when innocent he soon begins to look and act as if he were guilty of
what people accuse him of. Thus when the players act out the
murder scene before him and he discerns that Hamlet suspects him
of murdering his brother, he cannot help looking and even feeling
guilty, though he is not.

In his mind Claudius accuses Hamlet of wishing to be the
protagonist of a stupid tragedy and to cast him in the role of villain.
"He seems to have come into this world to perform a tragedy. His
education was for the sole purpose of constructing the plot, and his
philosophy serves to make it seem plausible."

Claudius tries to suppress the ill will toward Hamlet that rises
spontaneously in his heart, but he is finally unsuccessful. He hates
him now from the bottom of his heart. He sends him to England
and arranges to have him killed, since it is either Hamlet's death or
his own. When word reaches him that Hamlet is dead, he is filled
with a premonition of still more evil to come.

Here the journal ends, but Shiga asserts in a postscript that "the
fate of this Claudius is not necessarily the same as in the play
Hamlet."

This story is a tour de force, interesting because of its unusual,
and yet to some extent plausible, interpretation of Shakespeare's
play. It is interesting too because of the insight it gives us into
Shiga's psychology, since it is evident that he identifies himself with
Claudius.

In "Reconciliation" and elsewhere we have already seen Shiga's
high evaluation of all that is natural: his belief that man at any
given moment can only do what comes naturally to him; that

philosophy, ideals, rational thought can have little real influence on man's action. The following sentiments of Claudius give eloquent expression to this belief:

> My great defect is that my entire being is sometimes irresistibly attracted to a passing emotion and I lose my balance of spirit. It is not seldom that an early morning dream will upset that balance for an entire day. I am not the least bit afraid of what people may think of me. I know that there are more than a few that hate me. As long as I am dealing with such objective reality, I am not the least perturbed. I am not a coward in such matters. But there are certain feelings that steal into my heart and try to ensnare me, and in their presence my own heart becomes the most terrifying of all things. (II, 67)

> Isn't it only natural that I was not overwhelmingly saddened by my brother's death? To say that it is natural is splendid justification, at least as far as I am concerned. . . . Losing the brother that had been with me since childhood was certainly sad. But greater still was my joy. My heart is free. I cannot control it with my thought. I was certainly not pleased at this. But there is nothing I can do about it, is there? At the same time I suffer very much because of this condition. In this respect there is nothing that I have less control over than my heart. At this moment I stand more in fear of the uncontrollable movement of my heart than of Hamlet, who is trying to kill me. (II, 73–74)

In this story, therefore, Shiga—in the character of Claudius—gives expression to his own psychological state, that especially of the difficult years before the reconciliation with his father. From the point of view of craftsmanship and general literary excellence, this story is inferior to the others already considered in this chapter.

VII   "Seibei's Gourds" (1912)

Seibei is a twelve-year-old schoolboy whose one all-consuming interest is gourds. He has cultivated this interest to the point where he can discover potential beauty in ordinary gourds that others, even gourd-collectors of less discerning eye, would pass over as uninteresting. After school he wanders about town in search of new gourds for his collection, and at home he spends all his time treating and polishing his gourds, until they become objects of rare beauty.

But in this practical, no-nonsense world, such an esoteric art is not likely to find much appreciation. A typical reaction is that of his father's friend, who, seeing that Seibei passes over the old, gnarled, peculiarly formed gourds that generally attract collectors in favor of ordinary, even, and symmetrical ones, remarks to the father, "Your son seems to like only the ordinary ones," and advises Seibei that "there's no use just collecting lots of those things. It's not the quantity that counts, after all. You ought to find one or two really unusual ones." The father's own negative reaction is reflected in his reply to the friend: "Can you imagine a boy his age spending all his time playing with gourds!"

The most vehement reaction, however, is that of Seibei's teacher. Seibei had found one very ordinary-looking gourd that he was particularly fond of and spent much time working on. He kept it with him always, even taking it to school and polishing it under his desk during class. A teacher caught him at it during ethics class. Now this teacher was always extolling the classic code of the samurai and considered gourd-collecting an effeminate pastime. So, naturally, he confiscated the gourd, after heaping much abuse on poor Seibei's head. Still not content, he paid a visit to Seibei's home that evening before Seibei's father had gotten back from work, and announced to the greatly embarrassed mother that this was the responsibility of the family. "It's the duty of parents to keep such things from happening."

When the father heard about it, he gave Seibei a thorough beating, shouting: "You're no good! At this rate you'll never get anywhere in the world. I ought to throw you out into the street where you belong!" Then with a hammer he smashed to pieces every one of Seibei's gourds.

The day after this incident the teacher gave the confiscated gourd to one of the school janitors. This janitor, hard pressed for money, took the gourd to the local curio shop, expecting to get only a few sen for it. Surprised to find the curio dealer willing to give him five yen, the shrewd janitor began to haggle and finally walked out of the shop with fifty yen in his pocket, the equivalent of a year's wages. Little did he realize that the curio dealer, shrewder still, would sell the gourd to a wealthy collector for six hundred yen.

The story ends as follows:

Seibei is now completely taken up with painting. Now that he has found a new occupation he no longer harbors any resentment toward the teacher or even toward his father, who smashed more than ten of his precious gourds.

But his father has already begun to find fault with his painting. (II, 104)

Even without Shiga's admission that his motive in writing this story was "resentment toward my father, who expressed such great displeasure at my writing fiction," it is immediately evident that Seibei and his gourds are a literary symbol for Shiga and his writing, especially if one adverts to the time of the story's composition, December of the year Shiga left home. Here Shiga succeeds in giving objective form to his feelings of resentment toward his father, in a story which has the even symmetry and simple beauty of one of Seibei's gourds.

The story can also be read as a parable illustrating the essence of Shiga's art. Seibei has a keen eye for selecting his gourds, and the gourds he selects are invariably simple and ordinary ones. Shiga likewise has an eye for fastening upon the significant elements of ordinary human experience. Both prefer the simple and natural to the striking and unusual. After securing his gourds, Seibei works untiringly at them until their simple beauty becomes manifest to the eye capable of apprehending it. So Shiga, eschewing ornament and exaggeration, orders the elements of ordinary experience until their beauty becomes manifest.

Unfortunately, a story as simple as this loses very much in even the best translation, since its excellence depends so much upon its use of language. The setting of the scene, the limning of the characters, and the unfolding of the action are all done with great economy. The words are almost all concrete. The sentences are short and have a crisp ring to them. There are few adjectives; the main burden of meaning is carried by the verbs. Despite the wealth of nuance, there is no fuzziness anywhere.

The structure of the story is tight. We have seen the ending. The beginning runs parallel to it:

This is a story about a boy named Seibei and about his gourds. Afterward Seibei gave up the gourds and found something to replace them: he took up painting. He is now as absorbed in his new hobby as he had once been in his gourds. (II, 100)

With such clarity of structure we know always in what direction the story is moving.

The character of Seibei is most fully developed, but the other characters are also clearly conceived. The father does not understand his son or even try to do so. His ordinary norm of judgment is obvious in his criticism of Seibei: "You'll never get anywhere in the world." He is not uninterested in gourds, but in assessing their worth he is only too ready to rely upon the opinions of "experts." The Bakin gourd which he praises as "a real beauty" Seibei had found to be a big and clumsy monstrosity. When Seibei expresses his opinion, his father silences him with his authority: "You don't know what you're talking about, so you'd better shut up!" (Shiga states that the introduction of a Bakin gourd into the story was the result of the following incident: "Just before I went to Onomichi Father asked me what kind of a man I thought I'd become if I spent my life as a writer. I answered that Bakin had also been a writer but had written only stupid stories. I knew that he liked Bakin and had often read *Eight Dogs*. The fact is that I had almost no acquaintance with Bakin's work . . . [X, 175].")

The teacher is not too different from the father, but is even more ignorant. His world is far removed from the world of art. He is not only not interested in gourds—unlike the father—but even becomes incensed that Seibei should be interested in them. His bullying of Seibei's mother reveals not only his own crudeness and lack of culture but also the mother's weakness before the authority of the teacher. Even the school janitor—in just one line—is given a vivid characterization: "[When he was offered five yen for the gourd] the janitor was surprised, but being quite a shrewd man, he answered coolly, 'I certainly wouldn't sell it for that.'"

VIII "Han's Crime" (1913)

The story begins with a succinct account of the crime:

It was a very strange incident. A young Chinese juggler by the name of Han in the course of a performance severed his wife's carotid artery with one of his knives. The young woman died on the spot and Han was immediately arrested. (II, 114)

The body of the story consists of the examining judge's interrogation of the director of the theater, of Han's assistant in his juggling act, and finally of Han himself. The question is to decide whether the killing was deliberate murder or merely manslaughter.

The director testifies that Han's act is very difficult and requires steady nerves, complete concentration, and even a certain kind of intuitive sense. He cannot say whether the killing was intended or not.

The assistant tells the judge what he knows about Han and his wife. Han's behavior was always correct. He had become a Christian the previous year and always seemed to be reading Christian literature. Both Han and his wife were kind and gentle, very good to their friends and acquaintances, and never quarreled with others. Between themselves, however, it was another matter. They could be very cruel to each other. They had had a child, born prematurely, that had died soon after birth. Since its death their relationship had become strained. Han never raised his hand against his wife, but he always looked at her with angry eyes. He had confided to the assistant that his love for her had died but that he had no real grounds for a divorce. The assistant thinks that it was to overcome his hatred for her that Han had taken to reading the Bible and collections of Christian sermons. The wife could not leave Han because she would never have been able to find anyone else to marry her and she would have been unable to make her own living. The assistant admits that at the moment of the accident the thought had flashed through his mind, "He's gone and killed her," but now he is not so certain. It may have been because of his knowledge of Han's hatred for her that this thought had entered his head. He concludes his testimony by stating that after the incident Han dropped to his knees and prayed for some time in silence.

Interrogated next by the judge, Han admits that he had stopped loving his wife when the child was born, since he knew that it was not his. The child had died smothered by its mother's breasts and Han does not know whether this was accidental or not, though his wife had told him it was. Han thinks that she never really loved him. After the child's death she would observe him "with a cold, cruel look in her eyes" as he gradually went to pieces. "She never showed a flicker of sympathy as she saw me struggling in agony to escape into a better, truer sort of existence."

Han never considered leaving his wife because of his ideals: he wanted to behave in such a way as not to be in the wrong. When asked if he had ever thought of killing her, he admits that at first he often used to think how nice it would be if she were dead. Then, the night before the incident, the thought of killing her had occurred to him but never reached the point of decision. They had had a quarrel because supper was not ready when it should have been. He spent a sleepless night, visited by many nightmarish thoughts, but the idea of killing his wife gradually faded and he "was overcome by the sad, empty feeling that follows a nightmare." He realized that he was too weakhearted to achieve a better life than the one he had.

The next day he was physically exhausted, but the idea of killing no longer occurred to him. He did not even think of that evening's performance. But when the time came to take up his knives to begin his act, he found himself without his usual control. The first two knives did not miss their mark by far, but the third knife lodged itself in his wife's throat. At that moment Han felt that he had done it on purpose. To deceive the witnesses of the scene, he made a pretense of being grief-stricken and fell to his knees in prayer. He was certain that he could make others believe it was an accident.

But then he began to doubt that he had done it on purpose. Perhaps he had only thought he had done so because of his reflections of the previous night. The more he thought about it, the less certain he was about the actuality. It was at this point that he realized that his best defense would be admission of the truth. Since he himself did not know whether he was guilty or innocent, no one else could possibly know either. When the judge asks him if he feels any sorrow for her death, Han admits candidly that he does not, that he never imagined that her death would bring him such a sense of happiness. After this testimony the judge hands down a verdict of not guilty.

"Han's Crime," like "Seibei's Gourds," is a skillful objectification of Shiga's state of mind at the time of its writing. The story was written in the brief period between his release from the hospital after his accident and his departure for Kinosaki. Leisurely reflection at Kinosaki upon the implications of his encounter with death was to drastically change his attitude toward life and to mark a turning point in his work—away from the posture of confrontation and self-assertion to one of harmony and reconciliation. It is therefore ironical that in the person of Han, Shiga should have sung his most triumphant song of self.

Han suffers greatly from the hypocrisy forced upon him in having to live with a wife he despises. He is a man of unusual intelligence, great sensitivity, and an "overwhelming desire to enter into a truer sort of life." His feelings the night before the event are certainly those of Shiga himself at the time when he was determined to "mine" what was in him.

. . . I was more worked up than I had ever been. Of late I had come to realize with anger and grief that I had no real life of my own. At night when I went to bed, I could not get to sleep but lay there in an excited state with all kinds of things passing through my mind. I was aware of living in a kind of a daze, powerless to reach out with firm determination to the objects of my longing and equally powerless to drive away from me the sources of my displeasure. I came to see that this life of suspension and indecision was all owing to my relationship with my wife. I could see no light in my future, though the longing for light was still aflame. It would never die out but would continue smoldering pitifully. I was in danger of dying of the poison of this displeasure and suffering. When the poison reached a certain concentration I would die. I would become a corpse among the living. I was nearing that point now. Still, I was doing my best not to succumb. Then the thought came: if only she would die! That filthy, unpleasant thought kept running through my mind. "In fact, why don't you kill her? Don't worry about what happens after that. You'll probably be sent to prison. But life in prison would be immeasurably better than the life you are leading now. Besides, that will be another day. When that day comes, you'll be able to break through somehow. You may have to throw yourself again and again against the obstacles and with no success. But then your true life will be to continue hurling yourself against whatever is in your way until you finally die of the effort." (II, 121–22)

Kobayashi Hideo, in an early essay on Shiga Naoya (1929), cites the latter portion of the above passage as an excellent statement of

the basic form of Shiga's thought, or, more accurately, the norm of his action. He is never aware of the gap separating thought and action. Or else, if he does occasionally seem to take cognizance of it, it is only when his thought has not yet come ripe, and even then passion unfailingly jumps in to bridge the gap. For Shiga, to think is already to act, and to act is to think. To such a nature doubt and regret are equally absurd.[3]

At the end of Han's confession, the judge asks him, "Aren't you
the least bit grieved at your wife's death?" and Han replies frankly:
"Not the least. Even in moments when I hated her most, I never
imagined it would be so pleasant to speak of her death." Whether
by chance or design, Han has triumphed and entered into what he
feels is "a truer sort of life." This note of personal triumph was
never again to be sounded so loudly and clearly in Shiga's work.
The story that immediately follows this is "The Kidnapping," and
we have already seen the tone of pessimism and defeat that
permeates that work.

But if "Han's Crime" is an excellent expression of Shiga's state of
mind at the time of its writing, it is not for this reason that it is one
of the finest stories of modern Japanese literature. The excellence of
"Han's Crime" is due rather to the abundant life and individuality
Shiga was able to give to the characters of Han and his wife, to the
interest and tight unity of the plot, and to the masterful use of
language.

IX   "The Good-Natured Couple" (1917)

Of the motive for writing this story, Shiga states:

> I greatly admired Maeterlinck's "Intelligence and Fate." It made me
> realize how ridiculous it was to build foolish misunderstandings and human
> perversities into a tragedy. I wrote this story as an example of tragedy
> averted. Maeterlincks's work also had a great influence in moving me
> toward improving my relationship with my father, which for a long time
> had not been good. (X, 176)

Like "Han's Crime," "The Good-Natured Couple" unfolds
largely through dialogue, the dialogue between the husband and
the wife. It could easily be rewritten into a play with four scenes.

From the very first scene the keynote is that of harmony. The first
dialogue takes place on a quiet evening in autumn and the call of
wild geese can be heard outside. The wife is sewing and the husband is stretched out on the floor beside her, lost in thought.
Suddenly he announces that he is thinking of going off somewhere
for a month or so. Her reaction to this is unexpected, at least to the
reader. Her first concern is that he may be unfaithful to her when
he is away: "But you mustn't do anything bad." His answer is

equally unexpected: "I can't make any promises." In the exchange that follows she presses him for a firm promise to behave himself, and he hedges, willing to promise only that he will try to avoid the occasions of temptation. He admits that marital infidelity no longer seems as bad a thing to him as it had once seemed. She protests: "It *is* bad! It *is* bad!" The trip has now come to seem more of a bother than anything else and he tells her that he will give up the idea. Now it is she who urges him to go ahead with his plans. But he is firm. He really hadn't wanted to get away so badly in the first place.

In scene two a letter arrives from the wife's sister informing her that her grandmother, who has stood in the place of mother to her, is critically ill and that she had better come. The wife is reluctant to leave the house, but the husband is all solicitude and urges her to go and stay as long as it is necessary. She shouldn't worry about him, he will get along. He promises that he will behave himself in her absence. She answers, "I know you will. Still, I'm glad to hear you say it." The four weeks of her absence are passed over in a few lines and finally she is back home.

Scene three takes place on a peaceful, balmy day in spring. The husband is taking care of the chickens when he hears someone retching nearby. He discovers that it is Taki, the maid, and he recognizes the symptoms of pregnancy. Immediately he realizes that when his wife finds out, he will be the prime suspect. Though he did not touch Taki in his wife's absence, he does not have a very strong position from which to argue his innocence. Before marriage he had had relations with more than one maid, and even after marriage he had never had confidence that he could remain continent for any great length of time. He had even told his wife that if he should be away from her for any lengthy period, he wasn't certain that he would be able to triumph over temptation. She had accepted this at one time, but of late no longer seemed able to do so. His position was weak also because any number of times in those four weeks he had been strongly tempted to lay his hands upon Taki. What had finally prevented him was a deep unconscious desire not to disturb the harmony of his family life, and this desire had proved to be stronger than the temptation. But how could his wife help suspecting him? And how could he protest righteously against such suspicion?

In scene four he finally decides to confront her with the fact of

Taki's pregnancy. For the past four or five days she has seemed quite out of spirits. He enters the room where she is sitting, but she doesn't look up, even when he speaks to her. He knows then that she knows, and the following exchange takes place:

"Hey! . . ."
"What? . . ."
"What's the matter? You look so out of spirits."
"I'm all right."
"I hope so. . . . Have you noticed that Taki's been coughing as if she had to vomit?"
"Yes. . . ."
"What's the matter with her?"
"I told her to go and see a doctor, but she won't."
"What do you suppose she has?"
"I don't know. . . ."
"You *do* know, don't you? . . . It's good that you know. But I'm not the one. . . . I admit that I am capable of that sort of thing, but this time at least I am innocent." (II, 214–15)

She expresses her thanks to him and begins to weep. Her tears make him feel ashamed of himself, because even if he isn't the culprit, he had certainly had inclinations in that direction.

Then the conversation takes another turn:

"Now that I know it isn't you, I have nothing to say. I was waiting for you to speak. . . ."
"Then you did suspect me, didn't you?"
"No. I trusted you. But I was afraid to ask."
"See! You did suspect me!"
"No. I really trusted you."
"You're lying. Your 'trust' was nothing more than wishful thinking. But that's all right. You're very intelligent. I expected that you would believe me. But if you hadn't, there was nothing I could do to prove my innocence. It's a good thing that you believe me. Once you began to suspect me, you would find more and more reason for being suspicious, and both of us would experience a great deal of unpleasantness. I never tell outright lies, though I may come close to lying in jest. But as a matter of principle, I do not tell lies."
"You needn't say anything more. I understand." (II, 215–16)

The story ends with the two preparing to help Taki the best they can, to prevent her from doing "something foolish."

It is not hard to discern an autobiographical element in this story. In the good-natured husband's attitude toward sexual experience, Otsu Junkichi, Tsuda Kiyomatsu, and Tokito Kensaku are recalled. It is as much taken for granted that a man has to have regular indulgence of his sexual appetite as that he must have regular meals and a regular night's sleep. But that is the husband's view. The wife's is quite different. If the husband had indeed turned out to be the father of the maid's child, the wife might very well have committed suicide or at least fallen gravely ill. She gets very excited every time he mentions the possibility of his infidelity; and even at the end, when she is relieved to hear him vindicate himself, she is shaking so that she can hardly bring a cup of tea to her lips. Thus, there are two points of view woven into the story to give it considerably more dramatic tension than is to be found in most of Shiga's autobiographical pieces. In this story too, therefore, Shiga has succeeded in giving objectivity to his inner feelings. It is interesting to note that Shiga here was being a prophet, that eight years after the writing of this story, at the time of the Yamashina affair, his wife reacted in much the same way as the wife in the story, so that he actually feared for her sanity.

A great part of the excellence of "The Good-Natured Couple" lies in the skillful development of the two characters and of their relationship. The two love each other very much and in the course of their years of married life have grown well adjusted to each other. He is very solicitous for her and if he cannot always be faithful to her, at least he is resolved never to lie to her. His strongest bulwark against temptation is the fear of disturbing the harmony of their household. She for her part loves and does her best to trust him, but it is clear that always a doubt remains, though she does not wish to admit this even to herself. Thus, the story displays remarkable psychological depth.

X "The Apprentice's God" (1919)

Senkichi is a poor apprentice of about thirteen or fourteen, working in a shop that sells scales. He overhears the older clerks talking about a new *sushi*[4] restaurant that has opened in the Kyobashi section of Tokyo and thinks how nice it must be to have the means to eat in such places.

Several days later he is sent on an errand to Kyobashi. He recalls the clerks' conversation and is irresistibly drawn to enter a small *sushi* house. He discovers, however, that his four sen, all the money he possesses, are not enough to buy even one piece of *sushi*. A, a young member of the House of Peers, who has dropped into the same shop for *sushi*, observes Senkichi's embarrassment and disappointment, unseen by the boy.

A recounts this incident later to a colleague and the latter asks why he did not treat the boy to a meal of *sushi*. "He would certainly have been pleased, but I would have felt uncomfortable," answers A.

Several days after this conversation, A happens to come to buy a set of scales at the shop where Senkichi is working. He is surprised to see the boy there, but makes a quick decision to treat him to a feast of *sushi*. On the pretext of having Senkichi help him get the scales home, he takes him to the new *sushi* house in Kyobashi and pays the proprietor to set him up to as much *sushi* as he can eat. He does not stay to watch him.

Senkichi eats as much as he is able and discovers that the man has been so generous that he can come back for another meal later. The proprietor urges him to do so or he will be in an awkward spot with A.

Far from being pleased with what he has done, A, upon leaving the shop, is overcome by a strange feeling of melancholy and wonders why. His wife that night tries to reassure him, saying that he must have made the boy very happy.

After Senkichi returns to his store, he suddenly realizes there must be some connection between the earlier embarrassing incident at the *sushi* house and the good fortune of this day. The man must have been in the shop when he tried to buy one piece of *sushi*. But how had he known how to find him? The coincidence was all the stranger when he recalled that this was the very *sushi* house the clerks had been talking about. So the man must have overheard their conversation too. The more he thought about this, the more convinced he became that somehow or other the man had overheard the clerks speaking about the new *sushi* house. Otherwise why should the man have passed up all the other shops and entered that particular one? Yes, the man had not only overheard the clerks but had even read his mind. From there it was an easy step in logic to conclude that this "couldn't possibly be the act of a mortal. The man must have been a god, or at least a wizard. Maybe he was O-Inari, the god of harvest."

In the weeks that followed, Senkichi thought more and more about the man. Whether mortal or god, Senkichi felt a great gratitude toward him. Despite repeated invitations from the proprietor of the *sushi* house to return and use up his credit, Senkichi could never bring himself to do so. To go again would be the height of impertinence. The story ends:

> Whenever he was grieved or pained, he always thought of "that man." Only to think of him brought Senkichi a measure of consolation. He believed that "that man" would come again sometime, with even greater blessings. (III, 29)

In this story, too, the center of interest is psychological. Shiga depicts the psychology of the boy, Senkichi, and of his benefactor, the peer. The boy is seen moving inexorably to the logical conclusion that his patron is a supernatural being; and his life is made joyful by the realization that there is someone with much power who cares for him. At the end he is awaiting expectantly the god's next appearance with more gifts.

The patron, on the other hand, is overtaken by a strange feeling of melancholy after his action, and he reflects:

> He had felt deep sympathy when he saw the boy's pitiful appearance the first time. The desire he had had even then to do something for the boy had today been realized through an unexpected bit of chance. The boy was satisfied; he ought to be too. There was nothing wrong in making another happy. So by all rights he ought to be happy. Then why should he have this strangely sad and unpleasant feeling? Where did it come from? It was a feeling similar to the feeling one has when, unknown to others, one has done something that is bad.
>
> "Perhaps the source of this sad feeling is that while one part of me exalts at having done something good, a deeper and truer part of me criticizes and pokes fun at this feeling of exaltation. If I only had a more modest regard for what I have done and made much less of it, this feeling would probably disappear. . . . But at any rate I haven't done anything to be ashamed of." (III, 26–27)

Even after this feeling of melancholy finally leaves him, he cannot bring himself to walk by the scale shop, and he even stops patronizing the *sushi* house.

Why indeed should the man feel so melancholy after having performed such a good act? Shiga does not pursue the question further, but the reader understands the feeling, even if he too may be hard put to find rational explanation.

In a postscript Shiga states that he had originally planned to have the apprentice get the name and address of the customer from the chief clerk. But since the man had given a false name and address, when Senkichi went to look him up, he found at the address no house but only a small O-Inari shrine. Shiga felt, however, that "this would be a bit cruel to the boy" and decided to end the story where he did.

These words reflect quite clearly the lack of ease Shiga felt when working within the mode of fiction. He found it hard to keep his characters at a distance from himself. More significant still, he had the feeling of a man who is telling lies. To alleviate this feeling, he tries to let the reader know as early as possible what is going to take place in his story, as, for example, in both "Han's Crime" and "Seibei's Gourds" where he sketches almost the entire plot in the opening sentences. Thus, there is no deliberate attempt to achieve suspense, no strange turns of plot, no surprise endings. He could never have written a story like Akutagawa's "Hokyojin no shi" (The Martyr), where only at the end is it discovered that the "hero" is really a girl.[5]

CHAPTER 6

Toward Silence

A S early as 1919 Hirotsu Kazuo in a very perceptive essay on
Shiga pointed out how different his latest work—for example,
"The Good-Natured Couple"—was from earlier stories such as
"Han's Crime" and "Claudius's Journal."[1] It was not only the style
that was different, but the very stance of the writer was changed.
He seemed to be receding further and further into himself, to be
sealing himself into a private world of harmony from which all dis-
ruptive elements had been expelled. He had lost all interest in the
ugly, the discordant, the unnatural, the conflicting, even in activity
itself, and searched only for their opposites—for beauty, harmony,
nature, peace, and passive tranquillity. Hirotsu regarded this
tendency as regrettable, since a writer of such piercing intelligence,
purity of heart, and strength of character had still a great contribution to make but could realize his full powers only by facing life
directly and plunging ahead against all obstacles. While Hirotsu
found much to admire in "The Good-Natured Couple" and such
pieces as "At Kinosaki," he asked: "But is that enough? Is it all
right for a man like Shiga to remove himself entirely from the
stimulation of the outer world and remain locked up in the cozy circle of the hero of 'The Good-Natured Couple'?" Hirotsu ended his
essay by expressing the hope that Shiga would soon emerge from his
world of harmony and once again do battle with the outside.

Hirotsu's wish was never to be realized. Shiga lived on for
another half century but, except for a few brief excursions outside,
was content to remain in his cozy circle. His writing became more
and more sporadic and more and more limited in content until
toward the end it stopped altogether. In this chapter we will
attempt to trace the course of Shiga's descent into silence, to discern
its causes and evaluate its literary significance.

I *Shiga's Early Work*

To understand better the change that appeared in Shiga's writing after 1916 it will be well to examine the peculiar nature of his work up to that time. This will also serve to summarize the scattered critical remarks that have been made on individual stories in the previous chapters.

In the first part of his essay, Hirotsu gives a fine analysis of the predominant characteristics of Shiga's earlier work. He notes first that the stories take their matter from what Shiga has himself seen, heard, touched, and felt. Shiga treats only of what is directly related to him; in some way or other he is always writing about himself. His piercing eyes discover significance in moments and events that less sensitive writers would disdain to record or perhaps even fail to notice. Thus, a young boy's hesitating to blow his nose and his hopping on one foot down the veranda on the morning after his new mother's arrival (in "My Mother's Death and the Coming of My New Mother") give the reader in a few brief lines of description a clear understanding of the boy, the family, and the atmosphere of the house that morning. Likewise, the appearance, character, and feelings of Chiyo (in "Otsu Junkichi") are suggested in the brief passage in which, broomstick in hand, she chases after the dog that is chewing on the straps of her *geta*.

The description is always terse, direct, concrete, unsentimental; without ornament, exaggeration, or interpretation. The last point is particularly important. There is no philosophy of life or abstract structure of ideas informing Shiga's work, unless it be the philosophy of living each moment at highest pitch in absolute fidelity to reality and to self.

But if the writing is not informed by a philosophy, it is not for that reason lacking in a formative principle. This principle Hirotsu specifies as "a heart on fire with a zealous love of what is right." In the passage from Shiga's essay on Uchimura Kanzo quoted in the first chapter of this study Shiga professed to have learned from Uchimura "to love what is right and hate what is wrong." That he did indeed take this much away with him from his seven-year discipleship is clearly evident in his work. Hirotsu points out that Shiga's cold, penetrating eyes are always fixed upon the good and the bad, the beautiful and the ugly; and always making sharp discrimination between them.

The basic tone of his writing is set by his grave and piercing eyes, fixed unblinkingly upon human life. They are eyes too uncompromising to be satisfied with just discovering the beautiful in life. Shiga cannot look upon the contorted as if it were straight, nor upon the straight as if it were contorted. He looks at things without adding or subtracting. . . . Even if he tried to close his eyes and not to see, he could not. That's the kind of person he is. Whether he wants to see or not, whatever is there to be seen finds reflection in the eyes of his soul. Thus, while he discerns the excited sense of justice aroused in the three workmen of "The Just Ones," he also has a clear knowledge of their helpless and miserable feeling once the earlier excitement has worn off. Though a torrid flame burns in the depths of his heart, the vision with which he pierces through the phenomena upon which his eyes alight is always sensitive and coldly penetrating. Yet there is nothing in him of that attitude of scorn or derision often found in observers with similar powers of penetration. In its place is rather deep melancholy and compassion. This is proof that his heart is always serious and pure and his sense of direction unfaltering.[2]

Hirotsu goes on to state that Shiga has a profound understanding of the human heart. Of all contemporary Japanese writers he is the one that shows the deepest knowledge of both "the spirit of God and the spirit of the devil." He seems to know more about decadence than the members of the coterie that waved that banner. This understanding of the complicated aspects of the human heart is especially evident in such stories as "Han's Crime" and "Claudius's Journal," where his scalpel cuts deep. "With no trace of sentimentality he stares unafraid at what his cutting has brought to light." A special characteristic of this ability to smell out the evil and the false is that it is more a matter of instinct than of conscious endeavor. At times this instinct is so efficient and relentless that the reader feels oppressed, cornered, nailed down. This persistent bringing to bay of everything that is the least bit evil, unjust, ugly, unnatural—or even merely vague or out of harmony—borders on the neurotic. It is this quality in his work that critics frequently refer to as *keppeki*—i.e., fastidious, though the Japanese word has more nuances than the English.

From the above we can understand the reason for Shiga's extreme self-centeredness. Relying so exclusively upon his intuitions and without a higher scale of values to give direction to his thought and action when these intuitions were no more than the surface stirrings of the passions (as opposed to the intuitions of his deeper self), he often appears egotistic in the grossest sense of the word, as for example in "One Morning" and "Otsu Junkichi." But at the same time the "love of what is right" was so deeply implanted in him that it was eventually able to direct him to a warm humanity and prevent his self-centeredness from poisoning his entire system.

One last point made by Hirotsu is that Shiga, realizing the impossibility of forcing his feelings to submit to conscious control, had no choice but to wait patiently until they naturally took the desired course. What was forced and unnatural could only produce disharmony in the soul and could even provoke an explosion. This process of waiting for the ripe moment is seen in "Reconciliation," where Junkichi's reconciliation with his father takes place only after his feelings have naturally moved in that direction, and in the latter part of *Journey Through Dark Night*, where Kensaku must undergo the experience of Mt. Daisen before he can return to the old familiarity with his wife. It is this vigilance against destroying the natural course of things, concludes Hirotsu, that best characterizes Shiga's approach to life.

II *Shiga's Style*

The style of Shiga's early work cannot be considered in terms of technique alone but must be seen as the product and concrete manifestation of all those elements pointed out by Hirotsu. It is from this point of view that Sudo Matsuo treats it in his full-length study of Shiga.[3]

The first characteristic Sudo notes is that the writer does not stand at a distance from his object and look upon it disinterestedly. Rather, he is both emotionally and actively involved with it. The object, that is, is observed indirectly while the writer is engaged upon some action that deeply concerns him. Certain objects that enter into his vision when he is concentrating upon action remain in his imagination after the action has ceased, and these enter energetically into his work of creation. Shiga says as much in an essay entitled "An Answer to Nakamura Shinichiro's Question": "If the writer looks upon things with the aim of using them as material for his writing, he tends to see too much and this is not good. In my case, I find that I make use of only those details that I have observed almost unconsciously in the course of an action, and which still remain in my head afterward" (X, 161).

Commenting upon the above passage, Sudo states that the central element of Shiga's action (in this early period) is always that of living genuinely and intensely and in such a way that feeling and acting are perfectly joined. This is another way of saying that Shiga lives in complete fidelity to his intuitions, his "felt realizations." In such a process the details not only select themselves but do so in a particular order or arrangement according to a form that is active rather than contemplative. In putting them on paper Shiga does not so much recall them as relive them, and this with even greater vitality than in the actual experience (for such is the magic of art). It is not a question, then, of something like Wordsworth's "emotion recollected in tranquility."

At times the process of selecting the details has already taken place unconsciously before he begins to write. But more often he must note down many unnecessary details and make the selection—always on the basis of strength of impression—as he writes. Of this process, Shiga explains in his essay "Notes of an Apprentice":

When I begin to write, I first set down many useless details—useless in the sense that while they may have a necessary connection with the content of the piece, they are not necessary for its artistic development. Only when I am in unusually good form can I separate these off at the very start. But unless I get rid of them in some way or other they will disturb the artistry of the whole. Nor is there any danger that the piece will be less perfect for not containing these rejected details explicitly, since, though not directly expressed, they nevertheless insinuate themselves into the story, perhaps between the lines or even between the words. When this happens, when the unrecorded details thus achieve natural expression, the completed work, too, will have a great naturalness about it. (IX, 37)

The second characteristic of Shiga's style, therefore, is that only moments of liveliest impression are recorded, but in such a way that the other moments are also suggested and a strong sense of continuity given. From this follows the third characteristic, that the scene thus actively relived is presented as if it were in first-person, present-tense narration. Since the emphasis is always on the particular moment, vitally lived and even more vitally expressed, the plot of the story is not much of a determining element. It cannot be known beforehand how these moments of intense life will arrange themselves. Sudo points out the limitations of such a method of composition. No matter how pure, unalloyed, and pulsating with life the individual moments recorded may be, a literary work composed entirely of a series of such moments must always be like a mountain stream and will never achieve the volume and depth of a mighty river.

In the essay "Rhythm," written in 1931, Shiga attributes the ability to seize upon and express these "details of life" in all their vitality to the "rhythm" of the writer's spirit. He begins by referring to the great pleasure that results from contact with a human work that has been well done, whether that work be an action, a painting, or a piece of writing. One awakens to the realization that there is something in one's own self that corresponds to that work and one's spirit is deeply moved. What is it, he asks himself, that resonates through such a work?

The resonance we speak of has nothing to do with the matter or form of a work of art, but somehow transcends them. I like to call this resonating element "rhythm." . . . A work of weak rhythm, no matter how skillful its execution or how lofty its content, strikes a note of falseness and fails to impress us. In the case of a story, we can know whether the work has rhythm or not by the aftertaste that remains after reading. The basic question is that of the strength or weakness of the writer's spirit as he writes. This is all that matters. (IX, 12)

III   *Transition*

The desire for harmony, for merging self into nature, was from the first as deeply rooted in Shiga as the desire for self-realization. In fact, it is the tension between these two desires that gives artistic density and texture to the best of his early works. Had he possessed only the desire for self-realization, his pieces would have been more strident and one-dimensional than they actually are; and when he finally did succeed in achieving the desired harmony, his work was no longer of much interest except to a few devoted readers.

Nature seems to have opened herself to Shiga in an extraordinary manner from about his nineteenth year, when he was still in middle school. In the spring of 1902 on an excursion to Mt. Kano in Chiba Prefecture he had an experience of the beauty of nature so deep that he was able to recall his impressions vividly some twenty years later. In the essay "Journey" written in 1923, he describes the experience as follows:

I was stretched out on the ground near my inn. It was a very pleasant spring day. Suddenly I became intensely aware of the beauty of the scenery, of everything around me, far and near. This was not the first time, of course, that I was aware of the beauty of nature, but that day's awareness was something quite different. I had been coming to Mt. Kano every year for the past five or six and the scenery was very familiar to me, but that day it struck me as particularly beautiful and I was deeply moved by it. It was from that time, I think, that my eyes were really opened to the beauty of nature. Moments of great insight often come in this way. (XI, 86)

In the essay "A Journey in Early Spring" written in 1940, he recalls a similar experience two years later when he was on a boat in the Japan Sea.

That night the moon was full and the sky was clear and fresh after the rain. Unable to stand the smell of fish in the cabin, I ventured out onto the cold deck and stood there staring into the night. . . . I remained to see the day break. That was my first experience of the beauty of nature on such a grand scale. The rays of the rising sun shot up from behind Mt. Tsurugi and gave the effect of an eruption of gold dust. . . . Where the moon was sinking down over the Noto Peninsula the sky was of a clear silvery darkness while the gold of the sky in the East gradually grew into the light of day. (IV, 246)

In the sixth chapter of Part I of *Journey Through Dark Night* the above experience has become the hero's Kensaku going home after a night of carousing sees the dawn beginning to break.

Watching the light gradually move upward from the East, Kensaku recalled a similar daybreak ten years earlier. That autumn he was journeying by himself and from the deck of a boat on the Japan Sea he watched the beautiful flush of dawn rise up from behind Mt. Tsurugi, upon which a gentle snow was falling. (VII, 77–78)

Shiga was to make good use of such early experiences of nature in his later work, and though there was always a considerable time lapse between the actual experience and his account of it, the details of the scene are so deeply etched in his memory that he seems to be still observing them. Even as late as 1937, when with Wordsworth in "Tintern Abbey" Shiga could bemoan the fact that nature no longer produced "sensations sweet, felt in the blood and felt along the heart" and that his eye had been "made quiet by the power of harmony," he was able, with one last desperate effort, to complete *Journey Through Dark Night* by giving Kensaku the experience of nature that had been his over twenty years earlier.

As long as the yearning for harmony with nature met resistance, Shiga was able to write and what he wrote was of interest. But from 1913 the opposing attitude of active confrontation of nature and men and of struggle toward self-realization began to grow weaker and weaker until it finally disappeared completely. There were many elements responsible for this change, as we have seen. Among them were his happy marriage, his growing familiarity with nature and traditional Eastern art, the desire for reconciliation with his father and the reconciliation itself, the streetcar accident which brought him face to face with death.

In the essay "Idle Ramblings of a Man of Leisure" Shiga describes the change that came over him at this time and contrasts his earlier attitude with his later. He had read Anatole France's story "The Garden of Epicurus" some time earlier and it had impressed him greatly. France's story takes place in the distant future when the sun has lost its heat and only one man remains alive, the solitary witness to the centuries of cultural achievement. Then he too dies.

Reading this, I was filled with great antagonism to the notion of man's eventual extinction. That might be the fate of the earth, but it need not be the fate of man. Before that time, before the earth became unsuited for the continuance of human progress, man would have developed sufficiently to separate his fate from that of the earth. This was a very practical way of thinking, one that would make it possible to live with almost any phenomenon. If one accepted such a long-range view of human accomplishment, it became possible to find meaning in even the most disturbing of earthly phenomena. Everything could be attributed to the movement of the Will of Mankind. . . . I entertained these illusions until I was thirty-two or thirty-three. I was often in a state of high excitement over them, but just as often I felt great anxiety and dread, as if I might find myself at any moment falling headfirst into a deep ravine. Unable to continue much longer in this state, I began to make the acquaintance of ancient Eastern art and to become familiar with nature, to love animals and plants. As I gradually adjusted myself to these new interests, the earlier way of thinking left me and I reached an opposite pole. I was finally able to achieve peace of soul, and this peace has continued almost undisturbed for the thirty some years that have intervened. (IX, 149–50)

With regard to the way this change of attitude is reflected in Shiga's writing, a rather clear dividing line can be drawn between "Han's Crime," which represents Shiga's most triumphant song of self, and "The Kidnapping," in which his sense of self has fallen so low that it has to be artificially sustained and even then with little success. The latter was published in January of 1914, after his convalescence at Kinosaki. About the same time as "The Kidnapping" is probably the passage in Part II of *Journey Through Dark Night* in which Kensaku, on the night deck of a boat on the Inland Sea, feels himself "enclosed in some mammoth thing" and cannot "shake off the feeling that he was being swallowed up by this huge thing that surrounded him," a feeling that was not unpleasant but made him "feel puny and helpless." But Kensaku at the end of Part II—and Shiga at the time this chapter was written—was still some distance from achieving tranquil harmony with nature.

IV *Five Sketches*

For the next five years—from January of 1914 until April of 1917, when "At Kinosaki" was published—Shiga found it almost impossible to write and produced only five very short nature sketches. These sketches are not very important in themselves, but taken in sequence as leading up to "At Kinosaki" they give insight into the nature of Shiga's struggle toward stillness and harmony. These together with "At Kinosaki" are the crystallization of the meaning Shiga was able to discover in his encounter with death. In all these pieces Shiga finds in the fate of plant and animal an important clue to the fate of man. At their root is the unspoken conviction that plants, animals, and men are subject to the same fate; both live and die in nature.

The first piece, "Dragonfly," is a celebration of life doomed shortly to die. On a midsummer day, so hot that the flowers and plants in the garden hang heavily, dying of thirst, a dragonfly lights on a garden stone. It seems undisturbed by the heat. The author reflects that only a month before, it was a grubby worm crawling awkwardly through puddles in the garden, while now it has but the few brief days till autumn before it meets its death. The dragonfly flies off, but is suddenly set upon by another dragonfly. There is the sight of wing beating against wing as the two begin to fall toward the ground. But then the two become one and fly off higher and higher until they are but a speck in the sky. Thus the drama of life and reproduction is enacted against the backdrop of midsummer dying and certain autumn death.

In the next sketch, "Wall Lizard," Shiga, living alone at Matsue, finds a wall lizard in his room and decides to kill it for fear it will come back again. He picks it up with tongs, takes it outside, and tries to crush its head. After several blows he thinks he has succeeded: one eye falls out and the mouth is wide open. He leaves it for dead, but when he returns half an hour later the lizard is weakly crawling away. The author has an unpleasant feeling that borders on anger. He would crush it with his foot if he were not wearing straw sandals. He sweeps it into a gutter instead. Later he feels compelled to go and look for it, and not finding it, he imagines it coming to his room that night in its butchered condition. Fortunately, that day he would be leaving for Mt. Daisen.

Sudo Matsuo finds in this sketch an expression of the contradictions in the author's attitude toward life during his days at Matsue.

It is the author himself that kills the lizard. He feels a physical repulsion toward it. (In "At Kinosaki" he calls the wall lizard the most repulsive of creeping things.) This feeling is like a natural force that he can do nothing about. There is contradiction in the fact that both the wall lizard and his repulsion toward it are facts of nature. The lizard, even with a hole in its head, has a tremendous attachment to life. . . . Why did the writer, who published almost nothing during this period, feel compelled to write this piece? Perhaps it was because he found in the lizard's clinging to its life a reflection of his own desperate attempt to hang on to his at the time of his injury. And he may have seen in his attitude toward the lizard a reflection of the doubt and even distaste he had now come to feel toward the stance of rebellion against his father and his surroundings, and of desperate self-affirmation, all of which had characterized his youth until now. . . . It was just at this period that this doubt and distaste had brought on a complete impasse in his writing of *Tokito Kensaku*.[4]

Sudo's interpretation may be somewhat far-fetched, but certainly there is a great contrast between the author's irrational hatred of the lizard, motivating him to kill it, and his regret in "At Kinosaki" at having accidentally killed a water lizard; and this contrast very likely points to a change in the author's attitude toward nature.

The shortest of the five pieces, "Day of Storm," presents a dialogue between a mountain tree and the storm that assails it. The tree shouts out in pain, "O Storm! Why do you afflict me like this?" The storm, out of breath, is unable to answer, but when the tree asks, "Why must you rage on like this?" it replies: "Just hold on. This is painful for me too." Here we find the same contradiction as in "Wall Lizard": the storm persecutes the tree, the tree resists. Both act according to their natures.

In "Hermit Crab," the crab, which is accustomed to shed its shell as it outgrows it and search for an ever larger shell on the beach, finally reaches the point at which it is too large to easily find a shell that fits and it realizes that the time has come for it to die. It does finally find a shell that will fit, but it no longer feels like getting into it.

It felt extremely depressed. Its strength had greatly ebbed. It reflected that the time had come to die. It wondered why life had to come to an end like this. What puzzled it more than the fact of death was the source of its longing to be more than just a hermit crab. Why should it want to be more than it was? Its dreams of that earlier time when it still inhabited the *kishiyago*'s shell [the smallest of the shells] had long been fulfilled. Yet their fulfillment had brought it no happiness. They had never satisfied its craving. Now it gradually grew weaker in body and spirit. It could no longer move. Finally it died. (II, 169)

Scientists discover the dead crab and pickle it in alcohol, where its color quickly fades. It lies in the bottle, eyes closed, and face still expressing the despair and agony of its dying moments.

The hermit crab had tried to get bigger and bigger and finally, not finding the happiness it sought, it had died in despair and pain. In the same way, the writer, conjectures Sudo, began to feel that his desperate struggle to establish self was nothing more than the path to despair and fatigue. The feeling of Kensaku in Parts I and II of *Journey Through Dark Night* that man must go forward to solve the problem of his eventual annihilation is superseded by the negation of the crab as he faces death. Thus, continues Sudo, we see Shiga's previous trust in life wavering; but he has not yet reached the point where he can find peace in the notion of man's basic harmony with nature, whether in life or in death. He has not yet crossed the divide between the two attitudes, but he has reached the point where he must soon do so.[5]

In "The Mountain Tree and the Giant Saw" the tree has weathered over a hundred years and now enjoys complete freedom from anxiety. It has long passed the time when insects or knives or hatchets could cause it to fear. It is even thankful for the fury of the storms that have built up its power to resist them. Then suddenly the lumbermen appear and cut down all the smaller trees around it with hatchets. It watches helplessly as the workmen come with saws and begin to cut down the large tree nearest to it. Finally, two months later, the lumbermen appear again, this time with an even larger saw, and the tree realizes that its turn has come. The piece ends as follows:

It was surrounded by stumps. Looking at these, it became sad. Must all my efforts until now come to an end in this way? it wondered, and it recalled one by one all of the threats to its life that it had feared—first insects and small birds; then knives and hatchets; and now saws. When it had feared the birds, it had not yet discovered what a knife was. When it had feared the knife [carving words and figures into its bark] it had known nothing about hatchets. But more fearful than the hatchet was the saw. Just as it seemed that it had safely escaped all of these, it had finally come to know the reality of the giant saw. It no longer had the strength to endure. But at the same time, it felt neither anxiety nor dissatisfaction.

Still, looking over the past, it did not regret all the efforts it had made so vainly. In fact, it did not feel that the efforts had been in vain. It no longer felt any of the desperate anxiety it had experienced when it had tried to elude the first saws. Nor yet did it now have the same languid sense of security it had had before the giant saw had appeared. It felt extremely lonely, but in this feeling of loneliness it discovered a certain kind of composure. (II, 175)

This shows how far Shiga had already progressed in his contemplation of death. He had found a kind of balance or composure in the midst of a dark melancholy. This agrees with the description of his condition in a letter to his friend Satomi Ton two months earlier.

At first glance melancholy is the opposite of vigor, but actually it is a far more pleasant and secure feeling than that of lightheartedness. On the surface I seem to possess the lightheartedness proper to a man newly wed, but at a deeper level there is a reserve of quiet melancholy. It is rather on this latter that I pin my hopes. (XVI, 112)

V "At Kinosaki" (1917)

"At Kinosaki" was written less than two years after "The Mountain Tree and the Giant Saw." Still under the shock of the realization of how narrowly he has escaped death, Shiga encounters three faces of death while at Kinosaki. First, he finds a dead bee lying on the rooftop of a passageway, while the other bees, indifferent and undisturbed, go about their daily routine of activity. Second, while on a walk along the rivulet that flows through the village he sees a rat with a skewer through its neck swimming desperately down the stream with several children and a ricksha man throwing stones at it in sport. Finally, he himself accidentally kills a lizard with a stone. It had been resting on a rock and he had merely intended to startle it back into the river. These three incidents plunge him progressively deeper into contemplation of the mystery of life and death.

We know from his journal that these incidents actually occurred. They made such a deep impression upon him that he originally intended to incorporate them in his novel *Tokito Kensaku*. It is good that he did not write the piece at once but permitted his understanding of the experience to mature before it found expression.

In this piece Shiga shows a still greater composure and peace in the face of death than in the earlier sketches. He thinks of his own dying, but these thoughts now hold little terror for him. He realizes that death may come at any time, and he tries to goad himself on to accomplish the "things I must do." But his heart does not respond to this goading. It is strangely quiet, as if it enjoyed a friendly relationship with death. His reaction to the dead bee, for example, is as follows:

Whenever my eyes turned toward it—morning, noon, or evening—it lay always in the same spot and in the same position, completely motionless. It gave very much a sense of death. It remained there for three days. I found a tranquil peace in looking at it. It was at the same time a lonely feeling. It was lonely to observe the dead insect lying alone on the cold tile at the end of day when all the other bees had returned to their hives. A lonely feeling, but a deeply tranquil one. (II, 195−96)

The rain washes the body of the bee away, but the author continues to imagine the quiet it is now enjoying after its lifetime of work. "I felt," he writes, "a certain nearness to that quiet." He thinks that he would now like to write a sequel to "Han's Crime" describing the wife "murdered and quiet in her grave."

The desperate struggle of the skewered rat disturbs his composure again, but only because it reminds him that the quiet of death is often preceded by the terrible agony of dying. He realizes that he himself, despite the little fear he now has of death, would struggle in the same way to live (as he actually did at the time of the accident).

Then finally when he accidentally hits and kills the water lizard, he is filled with a feeling of revulsion. He identitifies himself so completely with the lizard that it is as if

there were only the lizard and I, as if I had become the lizard and knew its feelings. I was filled with a sadness for the lizard, with a sense of the loneliness of the living creature. Quite by accident I had lived. Quite by accident the lizard had died. I was lonely . . . (II, 200)

He knows that he should be grateful that his own life was spared, but he feels no joy at the thought. Instead he comes to the conclusion that life and death are not two opposite poles, that there does not seem to be much difference between them. This feeling grows as he walks back to his inn under the darkening skies of early evening.

Synopsized like this, the sketch seems very simple indeed. But what transforms this rather ordinary material into a profound meditation on life and death is the style. This piece is written in language that has the concentration, suggestiveness, and color of poetry. To give one example, the two adjectives *sabishii* (lonely) and *shizuka* (quiet) recur again and again. Sudo Matsuo in his analysis of this story points out that *sabishii* expresses a personal emotion that is negative, while *shizuka* points to something deeper—beyond emotion, more objective, and affirmative;[6] so that even in the dialectic of these alternating adjectives is enacted the author's struggle to emerge from his "dark night" to the light of a contemplative state of harmony and peace.

While "At Kinosaki" has no plot or drama, it does have structural unity and thematic development. A lyrical poem written in prose, it is rightly admired as one of Shiga's finest pieces.

VI *From 1917 to 1920*

In the same year in which he wrote "At Kinosaki" and "The Good-Natured Couple" Shiga was reconciled with his father and all drama disappeared from his life. He no longer had anything or anyone to confront. But harmony was not so easily to be achieved. For the next few years Shiga hung suspended between the old state of mind and the new. He could no longer summon up the sense of excited confrontation that had been the *sine qua non* of the best of his early writing, and he had not yet achieved the unperturbed calm of his later years. In a short piece of the following year, entitled simply "Fragment," he complains that he is in low spirits and without any energy for action. He cannot bear to continue long in such a state.

The only other piece he was able to write that year, "The Afternoon of November 3," begins in the same mood. It is a hot, humid, generally unpleasant day and he feels depressed. He goes to buy a duck and in the course of his walk finds himself in the middle of Army maneuvers, with soldiers popping up all around him. Shiga gives a fine description of the brutality and lack of humanity of Army life. Though it is only a practice maneuver, the soldiers have been made to march almost beyond the point of endurance. Wearing overcoats and carrying a heavy load of equipment on their shoulders, they are sweltering in the Indian-summer heat and have no water in their canteens to relieve their thirst. Some fall and can go no further, even under the corporal's threatening invective. Shiga finds the sight thoroughly unpleasant, and when he gets home with his duck, he cannot find the heart to kill or eat it. He gives it to a neighbor. Shiga has found Army inhumanity so revolting that in reaction he cannot be cruel even to an animal.

Sudo points out that Shiga becomes outraged at the inhumanity

of the Army conscription system, but inasmuch as it does not directly affect him, the sense of outrage quickly subsides. For Shiga at
this time the only reality was that of his private life; there was absolutely nothing of the crusader in him. Thus, the central focus of
the story is upon Shiga himself firmly entrenched in the nature of
Abiko. The inhumanity of Army life is just another element affect-
ing the tone of his life, no more significant to him than the unpleasant heat and humidity of the day.

In the nature described here is felt the stage that Shiga had now reached.
Though reconciled with his father, the new state of peace and harmony
with man and nature had not yet firmly taken root. Even the duck that will
not float erect but topples over on its side is viewed as an anomaly of nature
and strikes him as unpleasant. A nature characterized by such anomalies
penetrates deeply into the writer's personal life, giving it an unpleasant
tone. In exactly the same way, the inhumanity of the Army, symbolized in
the exhausted soldiers Shiga encounters along the road on his way to buy a
duck, touch upon his private life and he becomes momentarily excited, but
with no reference to the public issue involved. He is excited in the same
way as he is excited at the unseasonably humid weather and at the duck
that will not straighten up and float right. This is just another element disturbing the tone of his personal life, just another element of an unpleasant,
reprehensibly perverse nature.[7]

The only story Shiga wrote in 1919 was "The Apprentice's God."
The following February appeared "Day of Snow" with the subtitle
"Abiko Journal." In this piece the monotony of life and low spirits
of "Fragment" are relieved by the beauty of a nature clothed in
fresh-fallen snow and the intimate intercourse with friends.

Shiga looks out of his study on the eighth of February to find that
a light, powdery snow is falling and rapidly covering the ground.
With his friend K he goes out to enjoy the beauty. He reflects that
there is something aesthetic about snow. "The sight of it affords us
an aesthetic pleasure that in our ordinary moments we forget that
we have experienced." On the walk home Shiga defines more exactly the nature of the aesthetic pleasure afforded by such a
snowscape:

I took the path through the rice paddies. The pond looked as if it had been
brushed in lightly with India ink, and the opposite bank, which should have

been visible, was now concealed. Dried-out bulrushes with snow on their heads seemed to float in clear outline out of the dark background. Among the bulrushes at the edge of the pond had been left long, narrow boats which were covered with snow. It was just like a painting. The excellent *sumi-e* [India-ink sketches] of the East capture just such an impression. I marveled anew at their extraordinary effectiveness in representing this kind of scene. But it is not only impression that they capture. They manage to express at the same time the strong spiritual hold that such a landscape has upon our hearts. It seemed to me as I gazed at the nature before me that there is no other way of viewing such a scene than through the eyes of the *sumi-e* painters. (III, 34)

The exhilaration at this view of nature is complemented that evening by the joy of spirited conversation with close friends concerning art and literature. These indeed—nature and close intimacy with family and friends—were two of the resources that were to rescue Shiga eventually from his spiritual doldrums. (The third was his growing intimacy with the ancient arts.) But at present this day at Abiko was no more than an interlude. There were more depressing days ahead.

VII "Bonfire" (1920)

The same year, 1920, saw the publication of "A Certain Man and the Death of His Sister," "Manazuru," and "Bonfire." The latter, like "Day of Snow," also anticipates the stillness and harmony with nature Shiga was to reach at the end of his troubled years. This piece is one of the finest, if not the finest, of his nature sketches.

The setting of the story is Mt. Akagi, where Shiga and his wife spent the summer of 1915. The piece had been begun at this time, so that like "At Kinosaki" it presents an earlier experience from the vantage point of a later time when that experience had had a chance to ripen and had taken on new meaning.

The plot is very simple. Shiga, his wife, and two friends, named simply S and K, have been confined indoors by rain since morning. They have been playing cards and feel tired, bored, and keenly conscious of the stale air of the room and of having eaten too much and taken too little exercise. Someone notices that the rain has stopped and they all go outdoors, to be greeted by the scented, cool air from the mountain. Shiga recalls that the rain had stopped at just this hour the day before and that all had gone out and climbed trees—including his wife—to get a better view of the rainbow. He suggests that this evening after supper they take a boat on the lake.

When they get out on the water, they see that someone has built a bonfire on Bird Island and they go to investigate. They find the fire built up in front of an old kiln for making charcoal and a man, probably a gatherer of bracken, curled up asleep inside the kiln. They head for the shore opposite the island and decide to build a bonfire of their own. As the fire leaps higher and higher, they exchange stories of dangers that are to be encountered on the mountain—danger from poisonous snakes, danger from mountain dogs, danger from ghosts.

The reference to ghosts encourages K to recount a very mysterious experience he had had the previous winter. Returning suddenly and unannounced to his home in the mountains after a heavy snow storm, he had lost his way and had already begun to feel the gentle relaxation and urge to sleep that signal danger, when he saw two lanterns coming toward him. It turned out to be his brother-in-law and three ice-cutters who lived with him. They had been awakened in the middle of the night by K's mother and sent to meet K. So imperative had been her tone of voice that none of the men had stopped to question how she could possibly know of her son's approach, since he was not expected. She had awakened in the middle of the night absolutely certain that he was on his way to her and that he needed help; and that certainty had not wavered in the slightest during the long while it took the men to make their preparations to venture out into the cold night. The only possible explanation of the mystery was that K and his mother were so close to each other that she had somehow intuited his predicament.

At the conclusion of this mystifying tale, the four put out their fire and return home.

Let it be recalled that Shiga went to Mt. Akagi shortly after his marriage and while his earlier encounter with death was still deeply impressed upon his memory. On the surface he appeared, as he wrote to Satomi Ton in a letter previously referred to, "to possess the lightheartedness proper to a man newly married." His stay at Akagi was a kind of honeymoon and he enjoyed a pleasant intercourse with both man—his wife and friends—and nature. But at a deeper level, the contemplation of the meaning of life and death produced in him a "quiet melancholy" which he also found pleasant. Moreover, this sketch was completed after his reconciliation with his father and at a time when he had achieved a greater peace of soul and harmony with nature than during the days on the mountain. Thus, the density of "Bonfire" is due to the concourse and successful blending of these three states of soul—familiarity and lighthearted intercourse with man and nature, deep contemplation of life and death, peace after reconciliation with his father and close harmony with nature.

In none of Shiga's stories is there a more felicitous selection of detail than in this one. Each of the three states mentioned above finds just the right objective correlative. The first state, for example, comes vividly alive in the following description of what had taken place the previous afternoon:

The day before too the sun had come out in the afternoon and there had been a lovely sunset, made all the more lovely by a colossal rainbow that extended all the way from Torii Pass to Mt. Kurobi. All had enjoyed themselves for a long time around the hut. Since it was in a grove of oaks, they began to climb the tall trees. Hearing the men exclaim over the view of the rainbow from the trees, even my wife wanted to climb, so K and I managed to pull her up to about six meters from the ground. K, my wife, and I were in one tree, and S was in another. K and S decided to see which of them could climb the higher and they worked their way up to a height of about thirty-five meters. At that height K stretched himself out in a fork of the branches and called down, "This is just like an easy chair." Then he lit a cigarette and began to shake the branches so that they moved like a large wave.

At this point Ichiya, a mentally retarded boy with a face that seemed too big for his age, came along with K's second child on his back to tell us that it was time for supper. So we all came down from the trees. It was already so dark that without a light we had trouble finding the comb that had fallen out of my wife's hair when she was up in the tree. (III, 51–52)

But nature is not merely beautiful and men can reach a deeper bond of union than that of mere conviviality. The two stories K tells to the others gathered around the bonfire make this clear. His first story speaks of the death that is inseparable from nature. K's father, returning from night fishing, is surrounded by fierce mountain dogs—the same dogs that had attacked and half-devoured a horse—and has to make his way home through the water to escape them. K's second story of his rescue from death through his mother's timely intuition speaks of the mystery in which both men and nature are plunged. This is the level from which Shiga's "quiet melancholy" springs.

K's second story is really the heart of the sketch, for it speaks of the deepest communication possible among men and between man and nature. In the light of this story all the elements of the sketch—the convivial conversation and play of the characters, the fresh green of the mountain scenery, the scent of the grass after the rain, the gigantic rainbow, the smell of the lake, the stillness of the mountain night, the multitude of stars, the two bonfires—take on a new aura of mystery and come together into a new unity.

The final passage of "Bonfire" reflects the harmony of Shiga's state of soul at the time he completed the sketch.

For some time now an owl had been hooting on Bird Island. It had two calls, separated by a short interval. The bonfire had settled down into smoldering coals. K looked at his pocket watch.

"What time is it?"

"It's already past eleven."

"Shall we go home?" my wife suggested.

K sprang up and flung a still-burning branch into the lake. The branch flew through the air, leaving a trail of sparks. Its reflection in the lake gave the illusion that another branch was skimming across the water. When the upper and lower arcs met, the sparks suddenly disappeared and the night fell back into darkness. It was so beautiful that the others also picked up the smoldering branches and threw them into the lake. K skillfully splashed water onto the larger logs with the oar, until their fire too was extinguished.

We got back into the boat. The fire on the island was now dying. The boat glided silently around the island and headed for the grove of trees that guarded the shrine. The hoot of the owl receded gradually into the distance. (III, 61)

Neither critical analysis nor translation can do justice to this story, inasmuch as its excellence is less dependent upon content than upon skillful use of language. Here too the reader cannot but admire the poetic texture of Shiga's prose.

VIII Journey Through Dark Night I and II (1921—22)

In the next two years, 1921 and 1922, Shiga brought out Parts I and II of *Journey Through Dark Night* and began writing Part III. As *Tokito Kensaku*, the novel, as we have seen, was at first designed to be a purely autobiographical account of Shiga's discord with his father. Now that the discord had ended he had no inclination to pursue his original theme. To salvage the parts he had already written and go on to complete the novel, he had recourse to fiction: he designed the structure of the two "sins," the "sin" of the hero's mother and that of his wife, and into this structure were fitted the individual parts. Since it was never more than a convenient technical device, it is no wonder that it has so little organic function in the novel. Shiga's inability to continue the work without recourse to fictional elements is eloquent testimony of the degree to which the desire to "mine what is in me" had begun to yield to the desire for harmony and peace.

Apart from the new elements made necessary by the fictional structure, the first half of the novel is a reworking of the sections of *Tokito Kensaku* that he had already written. It belongs, therefore, to the period before reconciliation with his father. Part III, however, which he began the following year, clearly makes use of later material, and this explains the gap already noted between the troubled Kensaku of the end of the first half and the relatively relaxed and tranquil Kensaku of the beginning of the second. Shiga himself makes indirect reference to the change in his own psychology in "At Kinosaki," where he writes that the new feeling "was so different from my notion of the hero in the longer work I had been writing that I became discouraged" (II, 176). The "new feeling" he refers to is very likely that of the time of his convalescence at Kinosaki rather than of four years later when the piece was written. Thus, at the very time that he was trying to write his "heroic tale" of self, he was experiencing a growing feeling of familiarity with the stillness of death that was weakening his stance of self-affirmation.

It is interesting to note that Shiga in his present longing for peace and harmony found the prospect of writing about Naoko's seduction and its aftermath so unpleasant that he had to steel himself to it by writing "Tree Frogs," a story with a turn of plot exactly opposite to that of his novel. In this story too the hero's wife is innocently seduced, but far from feeling alienated from her because of it, the husband is more strongly attracted to her and even finds sexual stimulation in imagining what took place. This story affords another illustration of the emotional gap that now existed between Kensaku and his creator.

The story is overly contrived and not one of Shiga's best. Its defects, states Sudo, are attributable to the fact that Shiga was now comfortably settled in his private, harmonious world and that his sensibility had become flabby. In place of the vibrant vitality that is characteristic of his best work, there is manifested in this story an inclination toward an artiness that is quite removed from life.[8]

IX   The Yamashina Stories (1925–27)

Between 1921 and 1925 Shiga did little more than continue work on *Journey Through Dark Night,* and even this he had to stop when he approached the seduction scene. The more peaceful and unruffled his life became, the more difficult he found it to write. From the beginning he had required a certain state of irritation, a certain flush of excitement, before he could sit down to write. When this excitement was absent, he tried to induce it artificially, as in "The Kidnapping." In the short piece "My Temporary Dwelling" Kosuke, a young writer, tries to keep himself in bad temper, for otherwise he cannot write. This day he manages to become irritable in the morning and he does his best to sustain that irritation until night (the only time he is able to work). But to no avail. By evening he is in good spirits again. He tries to put down on paper the thoughts he had earlier in the day when he was excited and irritable. But even this will not work and he concludes, "I was excited when I thought about these things, but unless I am also excited when I write, the words remain lifeless" (II, 157).

There was now very little to excite Shiga. The tenor of his days in Kyoto, where he had moved in 1923, was too peaceful for writing. The following passage in "Kuniko" is undoubtedly a relatively objective account of his own condition at the time:

The peaceful, uneventful days continued. Peaceful and uneventful on the surface, but I felt them otherwise in reality. It was as if I had fallen into a swamp and, struggle as I might, could find a foothold nowhere. Escape seemed impossible. My life was doomed to monotony.

I bred goldfish and raised birds. In the winter with the skirts of my kimono tucked up I repaired paper-door panels on the sunny veranda, prepared compost for the garden, and planted dahlias and chrysanthemums in the flower beds. It was a life no whit different from that of an old retired granny. (IV, 60)

In such a condition Shiga felt the need of some kind of stimulus to bring new life to his pen. This seems to have been the principal motivation for entering into a liaison with the waitress of the Yamashina stories. And the affair, especially after his wife's discovery of it, did in fact provide the irritant he needed. The hero of "Kuniko" tells how the affair with the actress affected his work as a playwright:

As a result of my relationship with Yukiko I came to feel alive again. I found a kind of foothold to get out of the swamp that I had been struggling unavailingly to escape from for the past four or five years. I was able to take up my work again and find interest in it. I felt freed from the strange cooped-up life I had been leading. I was finally able to return to my work of writing. I decided to take this opportunity to complete the ambitious play I had been thinking about for many years. . . . I wanted to write something that would give me a sense of accomplishment. So I became completely absorbed in my work. This was something that I had not been able to do for a long time. . . . I became indifferent to my wife and children. Nor did I consider this bad. I forgot about my goldfish, my dahlias, and my birds. I locked myself in my study from morning. In the afternoon I went out for a walk and then returned to my work until it was time for bed. During this period I was never in a good mood. If the children made even a little noise, I shouted at them. When Kuniko tried to consult me about some household detail, I got angry and refused to answer. I was always angry. . . . From fatigue I became easily excited. (IV, 72–73)

In the aftermath of this affair Shiga again took up *Journey Through Dark Night*, which had been taken up and put down so often, and was able to complete it as far as the fifteenth chapter of Part IV, getting Kensaku to the top of Mt. Daisen. In addition, he wrote the series of stories about the Yamashina affair and several other sketches.

X   *Final Sketches*

From 1929 to 1937 Shiga wrote only three or four pieces of no great significance. In 1937 he wrote the final chapters of *Journey*

Through Dark Night. He was silent through the war years but began to write again in 1945. From that time until his death in 1971 he wrote some thirty-five sketches, none of them, with the possible exception of "Ash-Colored Moon," of any great merit.

About one-third of these final sketches are about plants and animals. Now that Shiga had established an almost perfect rapport with nature he no longer felt the urge to write about the complications of human affairs, but was content to live immersed in nature, quietly enjoying the beauty that surrounded him.

Shiga's description of nature in this later work is very different from that in his earlier. He is detailed in his observation and he records what he sees in sentences that are well enough constructed, so that he cannot be faulted from the point of view of technique. But the high merit of his earlier representation of nature resided in something far less tangible than detailed description. It was his ability to seize upon significant details suggesting much more than they expressed that gave such power and such an impression of life to his writing. Why was this vitality now missing? Why did his sentences no longer move the reader as they once had?

The vitality of Shiga's earlier style depended upon the existence of a certain distance between the writer and what he described. Shiga was still so far removed from nature that the life of the latter cascaded into his thirsting spirit with a mighty roar. As his own life entered into deeper and deeper harmony with the life of nature, as he became "dissolved in nature," such roaring movement was no longer possible. The thirsting eyes that pounced upon the life they coveted were replaced by the peaceful eyes that possessed that life. All tension, all sense of urgency, all excitement, all movement disappeared; only harmony and peace remained.

It is not surprising, then, that in the later work the distinction between man and animal, even between man and plant, becomes more and more obscured. We have seen that Kensaku at the end of *Journey Through Dark Night* reaches a stage where he no longer distinguishes clearly between what is human and what is not. In the sketch "My House by the Pond" Shiga grieves over the imminent death of a cat as if it were human. The cat has been caught killing chickens and is to be killed in the morning. All night long it sets up a mighty wail in protest of its fate and Shiga is moved to pity.

When I reflected that something breathing out there in the night would become a lifeless corpse with the morning, I felt terrible. In the still deep of the night there were only the cat and myself awake. The thought that one of our two lives was fated to be snuffed out brought a deep melancholy. (III, 129)

Again, in "Komono Hot Springs," Shiga, observing the operations of the gang that his brother has gotten involved with, tells a dog, "You're really a fine fellow," and looks out of his window at a caged wild boar and thinks, "Here too is a good fellow better than many men." Many other such examples can be found in these later sketches.

In a short sketch of 1957, "The Yatsude Flower," Shiga describes the stage at which he has arrived in his life and in his writing. When he was younger, he writes, he had devoted himself so completely to his work that he resisted even the legitimate demands that his family made upon his time. But now he has come to the realization that he did not come into this world principally to write. "First and last," he concludes, "what is of principal importance is to live well the one and only life a man is given. That in the course of this life I have also been able to write is only of secondary importance." He is now very much inclined to envy the fortunate lot of the painter:

Long ago I realized that while a painter is able to paint until he dies, a writer cannot continue to write so long. In the first place, writing makes too great a demand upon the physical stamina of an elderly man. Second, the troublesome complications of human affairs have gradually come to be most distasteful to me. But when a writer seeks to withdraw himself from human complications, it becomes impossible for him to write so-called stories.[9] In that point too the lot of the painter is far more fortunate. He need not depict on his canvas anything that he finds unpleasant. He can always turn to nature and freely paint whatever he sees to be beautiful. The painter is indeed fortunate.

I am now seventy-four years old and according to what I have written above should no longer be able to write. In fact, I do write an occasional piece. But almost unconsciously my writing has come to resemble a painter's sketch. I have no desire to write "stories." Even if I had, I could never get myself to return to the Babel of human confusion that I have grown to hate. After all, I did not come into this world just to write.[10]

The gradual assimilation of Shiga's literary art to the art of painting was no doubt influenced by his ever-growing love of traditional Oriental art and the view of life that it represents. Of his discovery of this art Shiga writes:

I first felt drawn to Eastern art at a time when everything in my life was a source of pain and threat, when my spirit was restless and exhausted and I was searching desperately for a place of rest. I was naturally inclined toward contemplation [sei] rather than toward action [do], and so I was drawn to things Eastern, which until then I had not paid much attention to. (IX, 64)

After moving from Abiko to Kyoto in 1923, Shiga spent most of his time visiting museums and temples. Art occupied almost all of his thought and conversation. This interest continued to grow, especially after he had come to live in Nara. The following passage from "A Journey in Early Spring" gives much insight into the Shiga of these later years. As he contemplates a statue in the Nara museum he reflects:

This statue has looked out upon all the storms that have raged over this country for some 1300 years. . . . It sees the countless troubles that beset our nation today. . . . In these 1300 years it has experienced the good and the bad. From this long experience it knows that when this age and its problems have passed, another age will come. . . . But in whatever age, it will continue to stand as it does now. . . . I don't know when our world will finally achieve its equilibrium, but it is perfect equilibrium that this statue suggests to us even now as we gaze upon it. (IV, 232–33)

Takada Izuho, commenting upon this passage, writes that Shiga has in mind an equilibrium that transcends both contemplation (sei) and action (do), an eternity that transcends history, an absolute that transcends all relatives. At this point Shiga's humanism is absorbed into an Oriental view that places its trust only in nature. Shiga has moved from the stance of fighter (tatakau hito), to that of searcher for stillness (shizukesa o motomeru hito), to that finally of mere observer (nagameru hito). "To this observer, society and ideas have meaning only as objects of observation."[11]

Not all of Shiga's later sketches are of nature. A good number of them are accounts of incidents of family life and of visits with friends. All discord has vanished and Shiga is now the genial patriarch presiding over a harmonious family circle, and he records many details of his daily life, most of them insignificant. There are also many reminiscences of the past, in which his grandparents, mother, father, other relatives, and friends are looked upon with the perspective that time can give. He professes now to see "the backs" of past events, to discern their real meaning as he was not able to do earlier in life; and he is displeased that the critics should place such a low value upon these later sketches, which in his opinion have a far deeper penetration than the work of his youth.

It is true that these sketches of his old age are far more objective than the earlier, that they do discover a new significance in past events of his life. But the most estimable quality of the best of his early pieces was the impression of vigor and life that they conveyed. Even the past seemed to be present to Shiga as he wrote; even third-person narrative created the illusion of being in the first person. Now the past is clearly seen as past. These are the reminiscences of an old man; and while they contribute to our knowledge of Shiga the man, they add no new palms to the achievement of Shiga the writer.

Takada Izuho, in a passage immediately following the one quoted above, gives this summary of Shiga's final period:

Except for the completion of *Journey Through Dark Night* and two or three other pieces, Shiga wrote nothing of merit in his later years. His life as a writer may truly be said to have come to an end with his middle period. . . . The Shiga of the final period is no longer a living writer; he is more like a Buddhist statue. His eyes are as clear as ever, and he has become one who merely observes. Near the end of *Journey Through Dark Night* we come upon the following sentences: "Kensaku did not speak. He merely looked at Naoko, as if he were stroking her face with his eyes. To Naoko they were soft eyes, overflowing with love—eyes such as she had never seen before."[12]

This, implies Takada, is an apt image of Shiga himself in his later years.

Shiga's silence is not without its positive aspects. In the first place, it was a clear mark of his integrity as an artist. When he had nothing more to say, he remained quiet. He was faithful to his "felt realizations" to the end. Whatever one may think of "sincerity" as a principle of literary composition, certainly there is much to admire in a sincerity and genuineness that has been carried to such a degree of perfection.

Shiga's silence is a clear mark also of his integrity as a man. When it came to choosing between his life and his art, he had no hesitation in choosing the former. Rather than disrupt his family circle by continuing to pursue his philosophy of self-realization, he chose finally to become the good husband, the good father, the good friend, and he never doubted the wisdom of his choice. That he was successful in these roles is attested to by the great love and devotion he received from those admitted into the innermost circle of intimacy.

There is still another value to be found in Shiga's silence. His works can be read as one whole, very much as we tend to read the works of such writers as Henry Thoreau and Thomas Wolfe. Indeed, there seem to be many Japanese who read him in this way. Thus the earlier works are enhanced by the knowledge of the harmony and peace that would eventually crown Shiga's struggle through dark night, and the later pieces acquire new meaning and tension when read against the backdrop of this struggle out of which harmony emerged. It is here that Shiga's complete sincerity and integrity become elements of greatest importance, since they are the conditions which make it possible to look upon Shiga's *opera omnia* as one integral work composed of many interlinking parts.

CHAPTER 7

The Achievement of Shiga Naoya

WE come now to the most difficult portion of our study: the assessment of Shiga's position as a writer and of his contribution to world literature. In the foregoing analyses of the individual works we pointed out what we found to admire in Shiga's writing: excellence of style, vitality of lyrical impulse, insight into the nature of life and death, keen sense of man's harmony with nature, artistic integrity, many-faceted reflection of the life of one man. A few stories and sketches, as well as certain episodes in the longer work, particularly *Journey Through Dark Night*, we found deserving of unreserved praise.

Still, judged by the usual standards of Western criticism, especially those of the New Criticism, Shiga's work may not seem to amount to much. If literature is conceived of principally as mimesis, i.e., the representation of reality; if its primary function—or one of its primary functions—is thought to be the ordering and interpretation of the experience of men, then it must be admitted that Shiga is indeed a very minor writer. The band of the spectrum of reality that he represents is very narrow, the arc of the circle of human experience that he orders and interprets very small. He is far removed from Tertullian's boast that *nihil humani a me alienum puto*.

From the beginning Shiga excluded from his life and work wide areas of human experience. His world was almost wholly solipsistic and subjective, the world of one alone. The social dimension was almost completely lacking—not only in the sense that he had no social philosophy, no notion of the individual's relatedness to society at large, but in the sense also that he had no real notion of human relations on the I and Thou level. In his earlier autobiographical work, relations with others are merely the arena for the proving of self; while in the later work he goes to the opposite extreme of merging with others in much the same way as he merges with

165

nature. In neither is there to be found a sense of the uniqueness of
the individual human person. The climactic point of Shiga's life and
literature is well symbolized in Kensaku's experience on Mt.
Daisen: Kensaku discovers that nothing in the world of men really
matters, that man is but part of nature and wholly subject to its
laws. Shiga's final years were spent in a harmony with men,
animals, and plants that seemed to allow for little distinction
between man and animal, or even man and vegetable.

In Western writers we are accustomed to look for and to find
some kind of idealism and intellectual content. Even the lyrical
poets are passionately devoted to one or another ideal—such as love
between man and woman, justice, peace, individual and social
goals—and find the spring of their lyricism therein. In Shiga,
however, there is but one idea, one ideal: follow nature; and this
ideal is not so much conceived and striven toward as something instinctive. "Follow instinct and all will be well." Fortunately, Shiga's
instincts were basically healthy and constructive, perhaps because
of the channeling they received during the long apprenticeship under Uchimura Kanzo, but ordinarily this would seem to be a disastrous path for a man to walk, disastrous at least for society if not
for the man himself.

It is not only Shiga's creative work that is lacking in intellectual
content—i.e., ideas of any kind—but even his diaries and recorded
conversations.[1] The latter would not give us the impression that he
was a learned man. What we find expressed in them—besides comment upon himself, his activity, his likes and dislikes, and his family
and friends—are subjective impressions. The best of these are
aesthetic judgments, as often on art as on literature; the worst are
irresponsible comments on people, events, and situations.[2] Though
he lived through one of the periods of greatest change in Japanese
history, very little of this change is reflected in his work and only a
little more in his diaries and conversations. He might as well have
been a medieval monk taking refuge from the complications of the
world in a secluded hermitage close to nature.

Since there was from the first so little of human experience to
harmonize, one might be tempted to question the significance of
the harmony and peace the writer finally achieved, and to find in
the finished Shiga something of the quality of the Japanese dwarf
tree *(bonsai)*. While admiring the beauty of its form and the skill

and patience that have gone into its making, one might still consider it something monstrous and prefer to it the less aesthetic lines of the naturally growing tree with its greater impression of life and wholesomeness. Did not Shiga, one may ask, give too narrow an interpretation to nature and so end up frustrating it? Did he not prune it to fit too constricted an area? Are not the elements he rejected or merely overlooked—human relations, individual and social goals, conscious striving for moral growth—part of nature too? Isn't Nakamura Mitsuo correct in calling Shiga's writing a literature of adolescence? Such a complete trust in intuition and impulse, Nakamura points out, is characteristic of early adolescence and generally comes to an end when the youth finally confronts the real world, the world of objective reality. For Shiga this confrontation did not take place until after the Yamashina affair when for the first time he admitted another person, his wife, into his thinking; and thereafter he found it almost impossible to write. Near the end of his study of Shiga, Nakamura makes the following summation:

In his work from the beginning, Shiga was either the narrator completely outside the action of his story, taking the attitude of a mere observer, or else he was the hero with other characters having no more existence than was necessary to give coloration to the hero's feelings. The result in either case was that he never really presented himself in the context of an external reality.

Since he did not view himself as exposed to the air of the outside world, he never took hold of his objective self. During his youth, when the image of the self of everyday life was in agreement with his ethical conceptions, this weak point never emerged to view. That was because for him the complications of the inner self presented to his spirit a drama that substituted for external event.

But when the inner drama of self was played out and maturity finally arrived, it arrived in a form that was fatal to him as a writer, absorbed as he had been in an unlimited affirmation of self and indifference to the outside world. Maturity for him meant old age. When the struggle within self comes to an end . . . the ordinary person shifts his interest from the inner world to the outer. But Shiga, perhaps because the struggle had been so intense, no longer had the strength to do this. It was too prodigious a task to observe and analyze self and to attempt to gain possession of self through action in the external world. . . . On the one hand, his spirit was worn out from the very earnest interior battle he had waged, and on the other, he was now too accustomed to the ease of ignoring the existence of others. He no longer had interest in anything except what concerned himself or his family.[3]

Nakamura is equally harsh in his criticism of Shiga's major work, *Journey Through Dark Night*. Because of the special character of the hero, or rather because of his lack of character, writes Nakamura, the novel has the same narrow monotony one finds in private exhibitions of second-rate Impressionistic painters. "When compared to foreign novels, of course, but even in the light of the ideals that have nurtured the development of the Japanese modern novel, this long novel—which I am tempted to call 'nonliterature'—is surprisingly stunted, the expression of a very special world." Then Nakamura quotes Masamune Hakucho's well-known remark: "If *Journey Through Dark Night* is the highest peak of modern Japanese literature, then modern Japanese literature is a very low range indeed."[4]

But all of the above criticism may not be entirely just. It is based upon the premise that literature must always be mimetic, the imitation of reality in the Aristotelian sense. Is this necessarily so? Western literature, it is true, has been predominantly mimetic since the time when Aristotle gained the upper hand over Plato. But could there possibly exist another kind of literature that is not mimetic, a literature that takes hold of reality in an altogether different way?

The possibility of another kind of literature with its own distinctive set of critical standards is suggested in a discussion of Shiga by four prominent scholars.[5] Three of the four criticize Shiga in much the same manner as above. Shiga's realism is very detailed but his lens is too narrow; Shiga's world is too cramped, closed, shallow, and allows for no drama; given Shiga's approach to literature, resolutions of any kind are impossible. Katsumoto Seiichiro summarizes the postwar critical dissatisfaction with Shiga when he indicts the writer for completely ignoring the feelings and experiences of contemporary life. "In our own muddied, blood-smeared, shame-filled experience of life, we feel no bond with the world of Shiga Naoya."[6]

Tanikawa Tetsuzo is the only one of the four to rise to Shiga's defense. Tanikawa compares Shiga's work, especially his later work, to the India-ink sketches (*sumi-e*) of the Muromachi period. Shiga, it is true, borrowed certain techniques from the Western novel, but the genre in which he writes is something altogether different. It is the Eastern tradition that is alive in him. *Journey Through Dark Night* is not really a novel, in the Western sense of the word. It is rather a kind of picture-scroll *(e-maki)* drawn from the point of view of the hero. If criticized from the Western conception of the novel, any number of pejorative judgments can be made about it. But this would be tantamount to requiring of a *sumi-e* the effects of an oil painting.

At the large national semiannual art exhibitions are always to be seen many huge canvases. Though they are very impressive by reason of their size, they are often empty of content. On the other hand, at small private exhibitions are sometimes to be found small paintings of almost insignificant objects that are genuinely pleasing. This is not to reject the notion of large canvases or to impose a limitation of size. If the large paintings are at the same time fine art, nothing could be more pleasing. But it is wrong to say that all paintings or all prose narrative must be of a certain scale. Even in the present age, continues Tanikawa, one can appreciate the beauty of a fine India-ink sketch or of its equivalent in literature. Shiga would undoubtedly have more admirers, especially among the young, had he written about social problems, as did Arishima Takeo, but his writing would not have achieved the same depth. Shiga knew his limitations and tried to work within them. The very narrowness of his lens was what made it possible for his writing to reach such a perfection. Shiga's work constitutes a certain kind of literature in the Eastern tradition. It has its own consistency and integrity and possesses something universal that will appeal to any age. Shiga's literature, therefore, is certainly not a literature of adolescence.

Tanikawa continues with his defense. Shiga is a writer in the Eastern tradition, not the Western. Neither his life nor his work is based upon the Western Faustian ideal of man; he feels no need to spend all his days tossed about on the waves of the human passions. Of classical Japanese writers it is Basho that he most resembles, though he has much in common with Saikaku also. The influence of Zen and of such traditional Eastern thought as that of Lao-tse is evident in his work and accounts for its simplicity, silence, and virtue.

The most fundamental element of Eastern tradition is pantheism, and Shiga's "rhythm" is basically pantheistic. The rhythm of the universe flows into the spirit of the individual. When that rhythm is strong, the individual self feels united to something that transcends it. Shiga's rhythm is almost always strong, no less in his postwar pieces than in his earlier ones. There is a way of living and a way of writing appropriate to each stage of a man's life. In the Eastern tradition both life and work tend more and more toward silence, this descent into silence being a necessary stage completing the earlier ones.

In Eastern tradition perfection of art has always been linked with perfection of life, and Shiga's growth as a man paralleled his growth as a writer. From his earliest days Shiga had a love for what is right and this showed itself in many ways. He refused to be ensnared by material possessions. He yielded his entire inheritance to his younger brother. Though he loved art, he bought but few pieces and these he inevitably gave away to others or to art museums. He had the love of simplicity of the Zen monk.

Tanikawa first visited Shiga in 1923 in Kyoto and was then already impressed with the splendor of the man. Tanikawa quotes the novelist Sato Haruo's account of a still earlier meeting with Shiga: "The eyes are the windows of the soul and his eyes seemed to flash out at me from a great depth. The moment I looked into them I felt strangely pinned down. There was in them a warmth of affection, but at the same time they were eyes that could not but observe whatever there was to be observed. For this reason they struck me as filled with melancholy."[7] Tanikawa feels that Shiga's development as a man is essentially connected with his growth as an artist, and that he and his writing inspire men and teach them how to live.

Tanikawa's critique opens up a whole new perspective for viewing Shiga's writing. Traditional Japanese literature at its best was never strictly a literature of mimesis. Without a philosophy of history, without a notion of a meaningful whole of human experience to which each individual part of it is related and from which it can derive a meaning, Japanese tradition could form no concept of the uniqueness of the individual human personality (upon which characterization is based) or of the significance of any segment of human life (upon which plot is based) or of the wide causal reverberations of human decisions and actions (upon which the development of the action in a literary work is based).

What the Japanese artist tried to do was to capture as much of the reality or life of the passing moment as possible. It was always the present moment, isolated from the past or the future, completely integral in itself. Ki no Tsurayuki, Kamo no Chomei, Yoshida Kenko, Zeami, Basho, Chikamatsu—however widely they are separated in time and however much they differ in the particulars of their craft, each sought to intuit and to express the reality of the present moment. R. H. Blyth is correct when he writes that the whole of Japanese art and literature is aimed at infinity, "but not through space, not through the horizon. It is the infinite grasped in the hand, before the eyes, in the hammering of a nail, the touch of cold water, the smell of crysanthemums, the smell of this crysanthemum."[8] The West tends to place greatest significance upon the fullness of being that will result from the process of becoming which man, taken both as individual and as race, now experiences. It is the terminal point of history that gives meaning to each momentary segment of it. The East, on the other hand, places greatest significance upon the fullness that can be discovered and experienced in each individual phenomenon. The present moment is meaningful in itself; it is grasped without reference to either past or future.

The conditions under which Japanese culture developed were such as to nurture this piercing intuition into the "heart" of things in a way that it has never been nurtured in any other culture. Moreover, the Japanese discovered a methodology by which this intuition could be progressively deepened and communicated, and thus root itself so deeply into the national culture as to become the experience of succeeding generations of Japanese even to the present. This is the methodology of the so-called Ways *(michi)*: the way of Zen meditation, the way of tea, the way of poetry, the way of flower arranging, the way of calligraphy, the way of archery.[9] Each of these Ways was really an asceticism "deepening" the heart and inducing the desired intuition into the depths of reality, into the fullness of being to be discovered in each object of nature. The following of the Way perfected the man as well as his art; life and work were basically inseparable.

This intuition or insight into the heart of being was not something static. Each age saw a new development of it; each age had to assimilate itself anew to it. Is it not possible, then, to view

Shiga's work as the assimilation of the world of the present to this same intuition, as the latest development in this age-old tradition? Did Shiga, perhaps, discover and develop a new Way, the way of modern prose narrative? This would certainly explain the secret of his power to move readers. It would explain, for example, why a story like "Reconciliation," which fails so signally in meeting Western critical standards, could be acclaimed so highly by Japanese men of letters. It would explain why Akutagawa Ryunosuke, just before his suicide, could write in his story "Haguruma":

I stretched myself out on the bed and began to read *Journey Through Dark Night*. Every stage of the hero's spiritual battle moved me deeply. When I compared myself to him, I realized what a fool I had been, and I found myself crying. But the tears brought with them a feeling of peace.[10]

In his critique of Shiga, Nakamura Mitsuo depends almost entirely upon Western critical method, as might perhaps be expected of a scholar who began his career as a student of Western literature. Kobayashi Hideo, the dean of Japanese critics and a man deeply rooted in Eastern tradition, takes very much the same view of Shiga as Tanikawa, and he makes use of quite a different set of critical standards from those of Nakamura. In his essay "On Rereading Shiga Naoya"[11] he states that when reading Shiga's work "the heart becomes quiet." Shiga has a "depth of heart" *(kokoro no fukasa)* that younger writers, for all their perfecting of technique, have lost. "The absorption of the latter in realism has led to their loss of reality." Shiga's realism is always under the control of his burning spirit; it is always impregnated with his own peculiar poetry, a poetry such as we find in the best of the haiku and *waka* tradition. Shiga's technique is very simple, but he has a strength and genuineness almost without parallel.

The best of realistic prose narrative comes to birth as a result of the deepening and purifying of our ordinary experience. There is no other secret. Realistic writers err in thinking that they can depict anything. They ignore the importance of the eyes of the spirit. . . . When we consider Shiga's works in the context of all the other literature that surrounds it, it seems so simple that it gives the impression of being the expression of a man that is always on the verge of silence. But who can mistake the depth of reality that is depicted there? This nearly silent man carries us to an understanding of the deep silence within our own hearts and exposes the diarrhea of expression in modern literature for the disease that it is.[12]

There are many other scholars and men of letters who take the same view of Shiga as Tanikawa and Kobayashi. For them Shiga is a writer steeped in the Eastern tradition, a man in the line of Saigyo, Zeami, and Basho. He is like the ancient masters of the Ways: through the asceticism of his life—an asceticism that consisted in a complete fidelity to self, in the rejection of everything false, feigned, ready-made, out of harmony—he succeeded in purifying and "deepening his heart"; and this purity and depth of heart appears in his writing to give pleasure to and inspire his readers. It is for this reason that so much is made of his sincerity, his genuineness, his "fastidiousness"—all terms that have but a low place in the Western critical vocabulary.

Unfortunately, there is no critical yardstick for measuring "depth of heart" in either men or literature. It can only be pointed to. Only the reader whose own sensibility has achieved a like "deepening" can make adequate judgment on the matter. In the best of traditional Japanese literature, heart speaks to heart with but the minimum intervention of matter and form. The haiku, for example, is like a code that can be adequately interpreted only by a receiver who is on the same wavelength as the sender; both poet and reader (or hearer) must be well advanced along the Way before the haiku will seem more than a mere picture. Here a foreign student of Japanese literature labors under a twofold disadvantage. In the first place, his aesthetic sensibility has been nurtured in quite another tradition and is unsure of itself in this alien corn; and second, whatever familiarity he may have with the Japanese language, he is not likely to have sufficient sensitivity to the nuances of expression to be able to pronounce judgment upon its effectiveness.

In the foregoing pages we have treated Shiga's work almost entirely as if it were a literature of mimesis and have used the critical norms proper to such a literature. Now in this final chapter we take cognizance of the fact that it is a literature of ecstasis[13] as well, and for such a literature our norms are not adequate. Moreover, if Shiga's work has any contribution to make to world literature, it is more likely to be in the latter sphere than in the former. Does that mean that our study has been fruitless? We think not. After all, it is not a question of two altogether different literatures, complete and distinct in themselves, but rather of two differing lines—perhaps we might name them the horizontal and the vertical—to be found to some extent in every literature. The West has largely developed the one and the East the other. To analyze one from the point of view of the other cannot but shed new light on the literature, provided, of course, there is sufficient awareness of the one-sidedness of such an approach. Moreover, our analysis of Shiga's writing has made clear the limitations of a literature that neglects the mimetic element and does not do full justice to the warp and woof of reality.

In a much simpler age it may have been possible for a man to cut himself off from his time, from society, from history, and still not suffer a diminution of his humanity. It may have been possible for such a man to confine his muse to the objects found within this narrow circle. But today such a posture seems anachronistic and irresponsible. So much of contemporary human experience that is of great significance has been left out of consideration that what remains seems overly precious and poorly representative of the scope of man.

At the beginning of the century the poet and essayist Kitamura Tokoku lamented that Japanese literature seemed doomed to sing forever of flower, snow, and moon, and could not rise to the richness of either comedy or tragedy; that it was outstanding in elegance and refinement but greatly deficient in seriousness and sublimity.[14] It is this same realization that has moved the postwar novelists to try to throw off the influence of Shiga Naoya and break new paths.

But if the traditional Eastern approach to literature is limited in its ability to grasp and represent the fullness of reality, the Western mimetic approach also has its limitations. While it has produced a literature rich in the horizontal insight into the nature of being in all its relationships, the vertical insight into the fullness of the being of the present moment has remained largely undeveloped. The Romantics and the Symbolists sought to cultivate and express this vertical line, but for lack of an audience ready to receive non-conceptual verbal communication (an audience such as was created in Japan through the asceticism of the Ways) their highest flights ended in confusion rather than enlightenment. Again, the twentieth-century novelists have attempted to break up sequences of time and place and thereby achieve a simultaneity of presentation that would give enriched expression to the present reality, but these attempts too have not on the whole been successful. Joyce's *Finnegan's Wake*, one of the best examples of this kind of novel, is unintelligible without a key.

The point, therefore, is not which of these two approaches to literature—mimetic or ecstatic—is the better. Each is good but incomplete. Rather than censure Shiga for not possessing the virtues that are found in abundance in Western literature, it seems wiser to imbibe from him the elements in which our own literature is deficient. It is at this point that real cultural interchange can take place. It is for this reason that we dare to assert that the writing of Shiga Naoya has its place in world literature.

Notes and References

Preface

1. Special Shiga Naoya issue of *Bungei* (December 1955), p. 68.
2. "A Few Comments on Translation from Modern Japanese Literature," *K.B.S. Bulletin on Japanese Culture*, No. 87 (Dec. 1967—Jan. 1968), p. 13.

Chapter One

1. Nakamura Mitsuo, *Shiga Naoya-ron* (Tokyo: Chikuma Shobo, 1966), pp. 36—37. This work was originally published by Bungei Shunju Press in 1954.
2. "Recollections of Uchimura Kanzo," IX, 219.
3. "My House by the Pond," III, 124.
4. "Conversations at Inamura," X, 261.
5. *Ibid.*, 262.

Chapter Two

1. *Japanese Literature* (New York: Grove Press, 1955), p. 95.
2. *Modern Japanese Fiction* (Tokyo: Kokusai Bunka Shinkokai, 1968), p. 60. This is a translation of *Nihon no kindai shosetsu*, published in 1954 by Iwanami Press.
3. Nakamura Mitsuo, *Fuzoku shosetsu-ron* (Tokyo: Shincho Bunko, 1958), p. 72. The pages that follow are largely a summary of the early chapters of this book.
4. *Ibid.*, p. 56
5. *Ibid.*
6. *Ibid.*, p. 7.
7. *Ibid.*, p. 58
8. *Ibid.*, p. 60.
9. *Ibid.*, p. 64.
10. *Ibid.*, p. 68.
11. *Ibid.*, p. 83.
12. *Ibid.*, p. 84.

Chapter Three

1. Sudo Matsuo, *Shiga Naoya no bungaku* (Tokyo: Nanundo Ofu-sha, 1963), p.23.

2. Nakamura, *Shiga Naoya-ron*, pp. 84–85.

3. Special Shiga Naoya issue of *Bungei, op. cit.*, p. 31.

4. This and the statements of Kobayashi Hideo and Eguchi Kiyoshi that follow are quoted in *Shiga Naoya* by Fukuda Kiyoto and Kuribayashi Hideo (Tokyo: Shimizu Shoin, 1968), pp. 154–55.

5. Special Shiga Naoya issue of *Bungei, op. cit.*, p. 45.

6. Edward Seidensticker, *Nihon sakka-ron* (Tokyo: Shincho-sha, 1964), p. 97.

7. From the Afterword of the Iwanami Bunko edition of the three stories, pp. 285–86.

8. Nakamura, *Shiga Naoya-ron*, p. 85.

9. Hirotsu Kazuo made this remark about Shiga in the essay already referred to in note 3.

Chapter Four

1. In a critical essay in the *Kadokawa Bunko* edition of *Journey Through Dark Night*, vol. II, p. 271.

2. Yasuoka Shotaro in the first chapter of his *Shiga Naoya shiron* (Tokyo: Bungei Shunju, 1968) gives a Freudian interpretation of the fantasy that became the starting point for the reorganization of this novel. Yasuoka's analysis is long and subtle, but he suggests that Naoya may have had more than filial love for his mother and that, identifying himself closely with her, he may have had a subconscious fear of his grandparents. Thus, the grandfather of the opening chapters of the novel may be his own grandfather viewed through the motive of fear.

3. Nakamura, *Shiga Naoya-ron*, pp. 155–56.

4. Hasegawa Izumi, *Gendai meisaku kansho* (Tokyo: Shibundo, 1970), p. 415.

5. Nakamura, *Shiga Naoya-ron*, pp. 138–39.

6. *Shiga Naoya*, a collection of essays in the *Nihon bungaku kenkyu shiryo sosho* series (Tokyo: Yuseido, 1970), p. 300–301. Professor McClellan has kindly sent me a copy of the original English manuscript and the quotation and paraphrase are from that.

7. Special Shiga Naoya issue of *Bungei, op. cit.*, p. 51.

8. Sudo, *Shiga Naoya no bungaku*, pp. 228–29.

9. *Taisho bungaku-shi*, edited by Yanagida Izumi, Katsumoto Seiichiro, and Ono Kenji (Tokyo: Iwanami Shoten, 1965), p. 70.

10. Seidensticker, *Nihon sakka-ron*, p. 99.

Chapter Five

1. *Tabi* are the socks that are worn with Japanese sandals *(zori)*.
2. Shiga is wrong, of course. Claudius clearly acknowledges his guilt in his third-act soliloquy:

> O, my offence is rank, it smells to heaven;
> It hath the primal eldest curse upon't,
> A brother's murder.

3. Special Shiga Naoya issue of *Bungei, op. cit.*, p. 22.
4. *Sushi* are rice cakes covered over with raw fish or rolled in seaweed. There are restaurants that serve only this.
5. In his essay commemorating Akutagawa's death, Shiga writes:

> I remember that I criticized Akutagawa's writing. . . . In particular, I asked why in "The Martyr" he did not inform the reader from the beginning that his "hero" was really a girl. . . . I pointed out that the plot was well constructed and very interesting, but that by [his] deceiving the reader as well as the other characters and springing a surprise ending on him, the interest in the story is all drawn to this gimmick, to the detriment of the other elements in its composition. I prefer to have the reader occupy the same vantage point as the writer. . . . Otherwise only the plot remains in the reader's mind and the other elements, however well executed, are forgotten, which is very regrettable. (IV, 36)

Chapter Six

1. Special Shiga Naoya issue of *Bungei, op. cit.*, pp. 27–34.
2. *Ibid.*, p. 29.
3. Sudo, *Shiga Naoya no bungaku*, especially the early chapters.
4. *Ibid.*, pp. 144–45.
5. *Ibid.*, p. 145.
6. Sudo Matsuo, *Shiga Naoya* in the *Kindai bungaku kansho koza* series (Tokyo: Kadokawa Shoten, 1967), p. 112.
7. Sudo, *Shiga Naoya no bungaku*, pp. 180–81.
8. *Ibid.*, pp. 195–96.
9. The word in Japanese, *shosetsu*, has a much wider range of meaning than the English and is used not only of Shiga's novels and short stories but also of his sketches.
10. *Shiroi sen*, a collection of Shiga's later sketches (Tokyo: Yamato Shobo, 1966), p. 76.
11. Takada Izuho, *Shiga Naoya* (Tokyo: Gakuto Bunko, 1955), p. 36.
12. *Ibid.*, pp. 36–37.

Chapter Seven

1. Two volumes of conversations with Shiga have been published:
Shiga Naoya taiwa-shu (Tokyo: Yamato Shobo, 1969) and *Shiga Naoya to
no taiwa* (Tokyo: Chikuma Shobo, 1970).

2. Nakamura Mitsuo makes mention of some of his postwar proposals:
that the Japanese language be abolished and French adopted as the
national language, that a statue be erected to Tojo to remind the Japanese
of the evils of war, and to stop preserving ancient art objects (*Shiga Naoya-
ron*, p. 9). In *Landscapes and Portraits* (Tokyo: Kodansha International,
1971) Donald Keene cites the following comment of Shiga after the fall of
Singapore: "The unquestionable supremacy of the Japanese Army, both
spiritually and technically, has astonished even the Japanese ever since the
outbreak of war, but we cannot but feel humble when we reflect that a
large measure of our victories, reported in such numbers that we cannot fully absorb their magnitude, is due to the blessings of Heaven. The conviction that 'Heaven is with us' makes us feel all the more humble" (p. 306).

3. Nakamura, *Shiga Naoya-ron*, pp. 218–19.

4. *Ibid.*, p. 91.

5. In *Taisho bungaku-shi* (Tokyo: Iwanami Shoten, 1965), a series of
discussions of the literature of the Taisho period, edited by Yanagida Izumi,
Katsumoto Seiichiro, and Ono Kenji. Shiga is discussed by Katsumoto,
Ono, Tanikawa Tetsuzo, and Honda Shugo from page 47 to page 103.

6. *Ibid.*, p. 70.

7. *Ibid.*, p. 57.

8. R.H. Blyth, *Haiku* (Tokyo: Hokuseido, 1949), vol. I, p. xiii.

9. The doctrine of the Ways is not, of course, of Japanese origin but is
Taoist and imported from China. But as with Zen, another importation that
was mainly responsible for the progressive refinement of these Ways, the
doctrine reached a higher stage of development and realization in Japan
than in the parent country.

10. *Akutagawa zenshu* (Tokyo: Iwanami Shoten, 1955), vol. VIII, p. 77.

11. Kobayashi Hideo, *Sakka no kao* (Tokyo: Shincho Bunko, 1961), pp.
46–66. The essay was originally written in 1938.

12. *Ibid.*, pp. 56–58.

13. We use the term *ecstasis* in recognition of the fact that this kind of
literature produces a kind of transport, a transcending of the limitations of
time and place. It is a transcendence, however, that is not dissociated from
the concrete particular. See my paper on "Mono no aware" in *Occasional
Papers No. 11, Japanese Culture II* (Ann Arbor: The University of
Michigan Press, 1969).

14. In the essay "Takai ni taisuru kannen" in vol. II of *Kitamura Tokoku
zenshu* (Tokyo: Iwanami Shoten, 1960).

Selected Bibliography

PRIMARY SOURCES

1. In Japanese

Shiga Naoya zenshu. 17 vols. Tokyo: Iwanami Shoten, 1955–56.
A new edition of Shiga's complete works in fourteen volumes (with an added volume containing letters addressed to him) is now being published a volume at a time by Iwanami. The first volume came out in June of 1973, and the date for completed publication is August of 1974.

Shiroi sen. Tokyo: Yamato Shobo, 1966. A collection of forty-three sketches, many of them written after the publication of the *zenshu* above.

2. In Translation

There is no collection of Shiga's work published in English. In French there is Marc Mécréant's *Le Samourai,* a translation of "Akanishi Kakita" and twenty-one other stories (Paris: Marabout, 1970). A complete list of translations into Western languages can be found in *Modern Japanese Literature in Western Translations: A Bibliography* (Tokyo: International House of Japan Library, 1972), pp. 118–20. Listed below are the English translations that are most available:

BELL, ERIC S. and UKAI EIJI. *Eminent Authors of Contemporary Japan.* Tokyo: Kaitakusha, 1930. Contains translations of "Araginu," "A Moorhen" ("Ban"), "Hans's Crime," "The Razor," and "The Apprentice's God."

MATHY, FRANCIS. "The Razor," in *Monumenta Nipponica,* vol. XIII, no. 3–4.

MATSUDAIRA, MICHAEL Y. "The Apprentice's God" translated under the title of "The Patron Saint" in *The Heart is Alone.* Compiled and edited by Richard N. McKinnon. Tokyo: The Hokuseido Press, 1957.

MORRIS, IVAN. "Han's Crime," in *Modern Japanese Literature,* edited by Donald Keene. New York: Grove Press, 1956; "Seibei's Gourds," in *Modern Japanese Stories.* London: Spottiswoode, 1961.

181

SEIDENSTICKER, EDWARD. "At Kinosaki," in *Modern Japanese Literature, op. cit.*

SECONDARY SOURCES

Fairly complete bibliographies of books and articles on Shiga Naoya and his writing are to be found in the following three books: *Shiga Naoya* in the *Nihon bungaku kenkyu shiryo sosho* series (Tokyo: Yuseido, 1970); *Shiga Naoya* in the *Kindai bungaku kansho koza* series (Tokyo: Kadokawa Shoten, 1967); *Shiga Naoya no tampen* edited by Nishio Makoto (Tokyo: Kokinshoin, 1968). Below are listed the books that have been most helpful in preparing this study.

AGAWA HIROYUKI. *Shiga Naoya no seikatsu to sakuhin.* Tokyo: Sogeisha, 1955.

FUKUDA KIYOTO and KURIBAYASHI HIDEO. *Shiga Naoya.* Tokyo: Shimizu Shoin, 1968.

HONDA SHUGO. *Shirakaba-ha no bungaku.* Tokyo: Kodansha, 1954.

IMAMURA TAIHEI. *Shiga Naoya to no taiwa.* Tokyo: Chikuma Shobo, 1970.

KOBAYASHI HIDEO. *Sakka no kao.* Tokyo: Shincho Bunko, 1961. Contains two famous essays on Shiga, one of 1929 and the other of 1938.

NAKAMURA MITSUO. *Fuzoku shosetsu-ron.* Tokyo: Kawade shobo, 1950.

————. *Modern Japanese Fiction.* Tokyo: Kokusai Bunka Shinkokai, 1968.

————. *Shiga Naoya-ron.* Tokyo: Bungei Shunju Shinsha, 1954.

NISHIO MAKOTO *et al. Shiga Naoya no tampen.* Tokyo: Kokinshoin, 1968.

SEIDENSTICKER, EDWARD. *Nihon sakka-ron.* Tokyo: Shincho-sha, 1964.

Shiga Naoya. A collection of articles on Shiga in the *Nihon bungaku kenkyu shiryo sosho* series. Tokyo: Yuseido, 1970. Especially helpful are the articles by Katsumoto Seiichiro, Tanikawa Tetsuzo, Fukuda Koson, Yoshida Seiichi, and Edwin McClellan.

Shiga Naoya taiwa-shu. Tokyo: Yamato Shobo, 1969. A collection of conversations with Shiga.

Shiga Naoya tokuhon.. The December 1955 issue of the magazine *Bungei,* devoted entirely to Shiga Naoya. Especially interesting are the articles by Agawa Hiroyuki, Masamune Hakucho, Hirotsu Kazuo, Kobayashi Hideo, Kawakami Tetsutaro, Kamei Katsuichiro, and Ito Sei.

SHINDO JUNKOO. *Shiga Naoya-ron.* Tokyo: Shinchosha, 1970.

SUDO MATSUO. *Shiga Naoya* in the *Kindai bungaku kansho koza* series. Tokyo: Kadokawa Shoten, 1967.

————. *Shiga Naoya no bungaku.* Tokyo: Nanundo Ofu-sha, 1963. The best overall treatment of Shiga Naoya's writing. Much less one-sided than Nakamura Mitsuo's *Shiga Naoya-ron.*

TAKADA IZUHO. *Shiga Naoya.* Tokyo: Gakuto Bunko, 1955.

YANAGIDA IZUMI, KATSUMOTO SEIICHIRO, and ONO KENJI, eds. *Taisho bungaku-shi.* Tokyo: Iwanami Shoten, 1965. Conversations on writers of the Taisho period, including a long discussion of Shiga.

YASUOKA SHOTARO. *Shiga Naoya shiron.* Tokyo: Bungei Shunju, 1968.

Index

185